T0323593

Cambridge Elements ≡

Elements in Pragmatics
edited by
Jonathan Culpeper
Lancaster University, UK
Michael Haugh
University of Queensland, Australia

LEVERAGING RELATIONS IN DIASPORA

Occupational Recommendations among Latin Americans in London

Rosina Márquez Reiter
The Open University – School of Languages and Applied Linguistics

CAMBRIDGE
UNIVERSITY PRESS

Shaftesbury Road, Cambridge CB2 8EA, United Kingdom

One Liberty Plaza, 20th Floor, New York, NY 10006, USA

477 Williamstown Road, Port Melbourne, VIC 3207, Australia

314–321, 3rd Floor, Plot 3, Splendor Forum, Jasola District Centre, New Delhi – 110025, India

103 Penang Road, #05–06/07, Visioncrest Commercial, Singapore 238467

Cambridge University Press is part of Cambridge University Press & Assessment, a department of the University of Cambridge.

We share the University's mission to contribute to society through the pursuit of education, learning and research at the highest international levels of excellence.

www.cambridge.org

Information on this title: www.cambridge.org/9781009507486

DOI: 10.1017/9781009206617

First published 2024

A catalogue record for this publication is available from the British Library.

ISBN 978-1-009-50748-6 Hardback
ISBN 978-1-009-20662-4 Paperback
ISSN 2633-6464 (online)
ISSN 2633-6456 (print)

Leveraging Relations in Diaspora

Occupational Recommendations among Latin Americans in London

Elements in Pragmatics

DOI: 10.1017/9781009206617
First published online: February 2024

Rosina Márquez Reiter
The Open University – School of Languages and Applied Linguistics
Author for correspondence: Rosina Márquez Reiter,
rosina.marquez-reiter@open.ac.uk

Abstract: This Element expands the horizon of sociopragmatic research by offering a first inquiry into the sociocultural norms that underlie the establishment and maintenance of interpersonal relations in a diasporic context. Based on accounts of the practices that Spanish-speaking Latin Americans engage in pursuit of employment, primarily gathered through interviews, it conveys the social reality of members of this group as they build relationships and establish new contractual obligations with each other away from home. The Element examines occupational recommendations as a diasporic relational practice. It shows how the relationship between the recommender and the recommendee becomes part of the value being exchanged in the interlocked system of favours that sustains the moral order of the group. As such, the Element offers new insights beyond the dyad in a globalised context characterised by social inequality.

Keywords: interpersonal relations, favours of access, diasporic context, occupational recommendations, moral order

ISBNs: 9781009507486 (HB), 9781009206624 (PB), 9781009206617 (OC)
ISSNs: 2633-6464 (online), 2633-6456 (print)

Contents

1 Introduction

This Element is the result of a life away from 'home', of a life mostly lived in London, where, for many years, I have witnessed the struggles for mobility of many migrants, especially those of Spanish-speaking Latin Americans with whom I have several commonalities, such as a shared language, cultural practices, and the challenges faced in trying to convert one's skills or qualifications into recognisable forms of capital in a new social landscape.

The mobility of Spanish-speaking Latin Americans, in line with that of other social groups in London, is evidenced by the fact that they have left their home countries in search of a better life and, in this process, many of them have often lived in other destinations before settling in the city. Yet, this geographical mobility stands in contrast with their lives in diaspora, especially as far as their socio-economic mobility is concerned. Most Latin Americans are reliant on co-ethnics to access the labour market – chiefly, the London niche market economy of cleaning and hospitality in which they are mainly inserted. This represents a segment of the economy that is predominantly not taxed or monitored by the government and characterised by increased casualisation and general precarity. Incorporation into the labour market is key to ensure inclusion in society.

Against this background, the overarching aim of this Element is to try and understand how primarily economic migrants leverage social ties and establish interpersonal relations within the social group to advance their well-being under contrasting social and economic circumstances. In particular, this Element examines interpersonal relations among Spanish-speaking Latin Americans in the London-based diaspora through the lens of a cultural practice I am familiar with as part of my involvement with Latin Americans in London over the years: how they broker each other's integration into the London labour market. The Element centres its attention on co-ethnic occupational recommendations and what their accounts of this practice tell us about the normative behaviour expected of members of this social group in exchange for what constitutes a favour of access. In so doing, the Element explores the cultural values that a group of Spanish-speaking Latin Americans reflect on and orient to in effecting occupational recommendations and considers how norms are resituated in the light of the structural conditions of a diasporic life in London. This is done in the context of life-story interviews conducted as part of a long-term, ongoing ethnographically informed project with Spanish-speaking Latin Americans in London.[1] This offers important information beyond the traditional elements of

---

[1] See Márquez Reiter (2018) on interviews as a locus for ideological work and Márquez Reiter (2021, 2022) on ethnographically informed understandings of (im)politeness and offence among members of this social group, respectively. See also Márquez Reiter and Kádár (2022) on moral

context that pragmatics has tended to focus on: in this case, the construction of the accounts gathered through the interviews, the linguistic environment, and the conversational setting where they were conducted. Insights from ethnographic observations and involvement with members of the group are used, where appropriate, to connect the accounts with some of the macro forces that influence them, even when they are not articulated but are, nonetheless, crystallised in the ethnographic material.

The focus on the practice of occupational recommendations allows us to capture the largely tense dynamics of how social relations are forged and reconfigured in a diasporic context as members of the social group rally around a primarily economic project. It offers a window into how interpersonal relations are anchored and shaped by specific times (time of arrival) and places (London, country or region of origin) and are embedded in inequalities (Urciuoli, 2016). The Element, then, explores the social side of pragmatics (Haugh et al., 2021). It unveils the behavioural norms that Latin Americans report to subscribe to and often contest in their accounts of relating with one another as they attempt to make a living in London. The accounts shine a light on the participants' expected roles and those of others as members of the social group and the moral order on which relationships are established and maintained. Some of the inequalities they face become evident in the interplay of resituated values to a local context where economic betterment and settlement principally inform the leveraging of relations for livelihood sustenance.

Within the cultural diversity of the city, it is common for migrants to have some connection with their co-ethnics, in this case fellow Latin Americans. The term 'Latin American' is used here in line with research and government official discourse (CLAUK, 2021; McIlwaine et al., 2011). It refers to economic migrants that hail from Latin America, a region that comprises speakers of Spanish, Portuguese, as well as other European languages such as Dutch, English, and French. This Element concentrates on speakers of Spanish only. The presence of Spanish-speaking Latin Americans is particularly felt in the boroughs of Southwark and Haringey, and in around Elephant & Castle and Seven Sisters, respectively (McIlwaine and Bunge, 2016). To put it into perspective, this social group is roughly similar in size to Chinese, Polish, and other social groups in the country (Office for National Statistics, 2011).

Migrants are differentially incorporated into the labour market by ethnicity (Wills et al., 2010). Spanish-speaking Latin Americans are largely incorporated

---

conflicts resulting from structural vulnerabilities, Márquez Reiter and Martín Rojo (2015) on language ideologies, and Márquez Reiter and Patiño-Santos (2017, 2021) and Patiño-Santos and Márquez Reiter (2019) on convivial relations among members of the social group and banal interculturalism, respectively.

into low-skilled jobs within the co-ethnic labour market in the London economy, thus hindering their inclusion into mainstream society. They work with or for a fellow Latin American, typically in what is known as elementary occupations, namely, in the cleaning and hospitality industry. Employment conditions in these sectors do not generally require the same language skills – in this case English competence – as other low-skilled jobs in the sector (e.g., messenger, waitstaff) and jobs can be potentially accessed by a fellow country person. Employment is, nonetheless, precarious (e.g., not pensionable or fixed).

Those without formal qualifications or institutionally recognised qualifications in the receiving society primarily contribute to the co-ethnic service industry. In this context, connections with co-ethnics with whom they share a language, and an economic betterment project, can be instrumental for making a living away from home. It is therefore no surprise to learn that migrants look for employment opportunities within their social group and that assistance is often provided by way of co-ethnic recommendations. It is interesting to note, however, that while there is a tendency to recommend fellow country people over other Latin Americans for employment positions, ethnicity alone or indeed the same country of origin do not necessarily merit a recommendation. An occupational recommendation is effected when the donor (i.e., the recommender) trusts that the beneficiary (i.e., the recommendee) is willing to accept precarious structural employment conditions and has commitment to hard work, often over and above what is officially required for similar jobs in the formal economy. In other words, the beneficiary must show good worker qualities which are implemented as a means to achieve productive outcomes (e.g., absence of complaints leading to potential further cleaning contracts). In this sense, therefore, a good worker is meant to continue the labour chain without upsetting the economic order and the livelihood of the social group as currently constituted. In addition, first-order contact recommendations (relatives and close friends) and other forms of assistance (e.g., taking someone in) differ from those extended to second-order contacts (acquaintances). Less is required, at least initially, to connect first-order contact beneficiaries, but expectations of optimally appropriate behaviour are often higher insofar as they are oriented to as unquestionably normative between family members, no matter how distant they may be.

New arrivals, in particular, benefit from a sizeable group of culturally similar others that is, nevertheless, largely inserted in the lower echelons of the economy. They are under unequal conditions to fully engage in the receiving society, economically, politically, and culturally and are highly dependent on co-ethnic relations. Many of the Latin Americans who participated in the interviews examined here came to the United Kingdom to study or for economic betterment but did not, or could not, extend their visas or work permits. Some are now British citizens given their length of settlement and time of arrival to the United Kingdom. Notwithstanding this, the cleaning industry figures in all the participants' lives in one way or another, as it does in mine. Indeed, experience in the cleaning and hospitality sectors is one of the elements that brings this group together besides a common language, geographical origin, and purpose. Despite my academic background, the so-called 'hard' and 'soft' skills I brought with me and being a European passport holder prior to Brexit, my own lived experiences in elementary occupations afford me a distinctive perspective to uncover some of the complexities of having to fashion a livelihood outside the mainstream economy.

On various occasions, Latin American friends mentioned that they, or other co-ethnics they knew, had secured sought-after cleaning positions (e.g., flexible key holder positions that pay over the minimum wage or the possibility of setting up their own cleaning company) by way of *palanca*. This was surprising to me for the practice of *palanca* is associated with nepotism and corruption, whereby the institutional or organisational power of the recommender is used to favour friends, family members, or political allies (Zalpa et al., 2014) by virtue of their existing relationships. This is often done without considering the skills that the beneficiary can bring with them. *Palanca* ('lever' – literal translation) entails the use of personal influence or having connections with capital to better one's prospects, albeit mainly in the political sphere. In line with work recommendations in London, however, *palanca* also involves leveraging interpersonal connections for instrumental purposes. In view of this, and Latin Americans' labour market insertion in London in the lower echelons of the economy, what might the relationship be, if any, between the co-ethnic work recommendations in London examined in this Element and *palanca*? Both occupational recommendations and *palanca* involve the provision of a favour or the action of providing a connection (Starr, 2003) by a donor to a beneficiary, based on personal, in-group, and favour-based relationships. However, the positions achieved through these favours of access are markedly different. Unlike positions gained through *palanca*, co-ethnic work recommendations in London mainly lead to the beneficiary's incorporation into the informal economy with limited socio-economic mobility and inclusion into the wider society.

Co-ethnic occupational recommendations are understood as a situated and relational practice. The practice is examined here as discursively constructed by a group of principally Colombian participants through interviews. The participants' accounts of work recommendations shed light on the way in which cultural expectations, and the social norms that underlie work recommendations, are considered by members of this social group in the light of the structural conditions they inhabit, and the extent to which elements of the practice may relate to the practice of *palanca* back home. This is done by taking into account their historical and current circumstances – chiefly, their economic and different histories of migration. As explained in Section 3, Colombians constitute the largest Spanish-speaking Latin American group in London and have a strong presence in the areas of the capital where the research was conducted. Notwithstanding this, the term 'Latin American' is used throughout and, when relevant in their stories, the participant's place of origin is employed. This is because the conditions of having to make a living in the London niche market economy, where members of the social group are mainly inserted, is not defined by essential national affiliations or by a set of individuals in a given diasporic group (Hall, 1990). Despite the heterogeneity, diversity, and differences among Latin Americans in London, the structural conditions they face means that 'movement ceases and [...] their identities and explanations cohere – however momentarily' (Alexander, 2017: 1544). The normative orientation, the values embedded in the occupational mobility stories gathered and their relation to the contextual conditions of having to make a living in London are discussed. This contextual information is essential to understand the observed evaluation of the behaviour of others and of their own for it 'cannot be detached from the conditions of the real world in which it takes place' (Ortner, 2016: 47). Understanding these circumstances allows us to raise awareness and shed light on how relationships are established and maintained in a group that lives at the interstices of mainstream society.

Why should this matter to sociopragmaticists?

A pervasive condition of modernity is the movement of people and their detachment from territorialised interpersonal relations (Giddens, 1990). Over the last two decades, the consequences of migration have moved from the relative margins to the core of politics and global societal change. Issues about movement, mobility, and the increasing cultural and linguistic diversity that this brings are now seen as important challenges to how people live with one another. Yet, this condition and the communicative practices that diasporic members engage in to establish and maintain new and existing interpersonal relationships have largely escaped attention in pragmatics.[2] This is especially the case of economic migrants who have been incorporated into the informal economy of the receiving society by leveraging relations among members of the same social group and are, as a result, interlocked in a system of favours within that group.

---

[2] Though see, for example, Verschueren (2008) on (intercultural) communication in contexts of migration and Kirilova and Angouri (2017) on workplace communication practices in multilingual and multinational workplaces within the formal economy.

Through life-story interviews (Atkinson, 1988) (see Section 3) as part of ongoing ethnographic fieldwork, the Element examines reflective accounts of the occupational practices that a group of Spanish-speaking Latin Americans engage in to sustain a livelihood away from home. It shows how the practice of work recommendations among Spanish-speaking Latin Americans responds to historical and current migration circumstances, chiefly, their origins, history of settlement, and the economic conditions of a diasporic life in London. This, in turn, allows us to capture how the practice of work recommendations supports co-ethnic relationship maintenance as well as wider relations within the social group. In other words, the Element illustrates how dyadic relationships are sustained through reciprocal acts, whereby the favour of access (i.e., work recommendation) which had been granted needs to be fulfilled by socially normative behaviour regarding expected work ethics. It argues that such behaviour, in turn, supports relationship maintenance with the donor (i.e., recommender) and simultaneously supports the relating capabilities of the recommender with others within the social group, including those of the beneficiary (i.e., recommendee).

The dynamics of relationship building and maintenance is, then, centred on the situated practice of work recommendations and normative behavioural expectations of a wider participant base rather than the interpersonal dyad where pragmatics, and especially research on linguistic (im)politeness, has mainly concentrated on (see, for example, Arundale, 2020; Culpeper and Tantucci, 2021; Locher and Graham, 2010). This is not to suggest that questions of (im)politeness may not have any bearing on the participants' stories or indeed on their lived experiences in diaspora, but they occupy a second order given the principally transactional order, the realm of exchange with its own set of symbolic meanings and moral assumptions (Vivanco, 2018), that underlies relationships within the group.

The Element connects pragmatics with associated social science disciplines, such as sociolinguistics, cultural anthropology, and more largely migration studies. It considers how contemporary shifts in understanding the world as fluid and in motion (Sheller and Urry, 2004, 2006) can and should explicitly influence the pragmatics agenda. This means recognising that the sociocultural practice of relationality examined here represents a practice of (im)mobility. That the practice is not rooted to one place or location, and that to comprehend it and delimit its value in the social reality of the participants of this study, the larger contextual conditions in which it is embedded need to be considered. To this end, the Element shows how ethnographically informed knowledge and open-ended interviews, which are typically conducted as part of such fieldwork, allow us to give primacy to the configuration of relations between members of under-represented social groups who have been largely neglected in pragmatics, even when these factors are not necessarily evidenced in discourse.

Rather than taking culture (including the language of the participants in the settings examined) as a given entity by virtue of the comparability or cultural translatability of the communicative arenas examined (e.g., educational contexts, for-profit contexts, televised data, etc.) or taking the participants' native-speakerness or country of origin as an unequivocal point of departure, fieldwork allows us to attest important differences between participants, the interpersonal relationships they forge, and the dynamic nature of the practices they engage in. Instead of conceptualising the research participants via bounded categories, such as sharing a more or less fixed basic language or simply seeing them as economic migrants, it considers their different migration trajectories, the conditions they inhabit in diaspora, and takes into account important factors, such as their history of settlement in the receiving society. This, in turn, can help us to better comprehend the complexity of the interpersonal relations of the members of the social group observed, their structures and the value and importance of the practices they are able to engage in to sustain relational connections with one another, including the rights and obligations that accrue in a new context away from home.

A general discursive analysis of the accounts obtained in the interviews is taken to examine the norms of behaviour which members of this social group report to be expected in their daily interactions with co-ethnics for occupational mobility purposes. This is done by considering the structural conditions of the sector of the economy in which members of this social group are inserted and exploring its potential relation to the sociocultural practice of *palanca*.

The subject of this Element naturally lies at the intersection of the linguistic and social concerns that the participants make relevant in their accounts. In these, they attempt to make sense of the behaviour of co-ethnics by sanctioning it or condemning it in the light of what they deem to be appropriate sociocultural norms in the context of having to sustain their livelihoods in their new reality of life away from home. This research inevitably broadens the scope of socio-pragmatics (e.g., Culpeper, 2021; Thomas, 1983). It draws on migration and diasporic studies to understand the process of migration of the participants of the study, including geography (e.g., de Haas et al., 2020; Massey et al., 1998; Sheller and Urry, 2006) to comprehend the way in which they are inserted into the receiving society by way of their incorporation into the labour market, and cultural anthropology and communication studies on the sociocultural practice of *palanca* (e.g., Fitch, 1998; García, 2016; O'Rourke and Tuleja, 2009).

From a disciplinary perspective, the Element offers an invitation for pragmaticists to reflect on the societal impact of the discipline and to speak to current global challenges. This includes the discipline's much-needed expansion beyond its middle-class milieu (Márquez Reiter, 2021; Mills, 2017). This is achieved here by reporting some of the voices of those who are underrepresented and have rarely been studied in pragmatics, demonstrating how some of the categories typically employed in sociopragmatics, such as the notion of speakers of a given language, or explanatory factors, such as the familiarity between speakers or differences in power between them, are complex, fluid, and often respond to the structural conditions in which they live. In the case of this study, the power possessed and yielded over the recommendees has been mainly accrued on the basis of length of settlement, the resources recommenders could avail themselves of contingent on their time of arrival, and the connections they have managed to establish based on the normative behavioural expectations of the sector of the economy where they are inserted.

The Element is organised as follows. Section 2 is concerned with defining what I term the pragmatics of diasporic relationships, that is, co-ethnic relationships primarily established within the London-based diaspora. It highlights its importance in this day and age and explains its interdisciplinary nature. The section also contains a definition of the sociocultural practice of *palanca* based on extant research conducted on this sociocultural practice with a view to exploring its potential connection to work recommendations in a context of (im)mobility and economic migration. Section 3 provides the background and methods of the study. This is followed by Section 4, where a case study of work recommendations is presented. Finally, in Section 5, the conclusions of the study are offered, including a brief discussion of the role that sociopragmatics could play in examining contemporary communicative contexts embedded in social inequalities.

2 Towards a Pragmatics of Diasporic Relationships

The process of migration and settlement away from home represents a disruption from everyday life and everyday sociality. Among others, it impacts on how interpersonal relationships are forged and maintained in an unfamiliar sociocultural environment as well as back home. This is especially relevant though not limited to migrants who arrive with no or few social connections in culturally similar social groups in the host society or in the wider receiving society. These migrants typically look for co-nationals, co-ethnics, or a diasporic group to help them navigate in an unknown landscape

(Boyd, 1989; Massey et al., 1998).[3] This is precisely the case of the participants of this study: economic migrants who, by and large, have limited cultural capital (Bourdieu 1986), that is, knowledge and skills, including (higher) educational qualifications which are officially recognised in the receiving society or possess sufficient knowledge of the majority language to feel comfortable and confident in using it. This, in turn, leads to their dependency, at least initially, on co-ethnic connections.

While issues of migrant employability continue to receive extensive attention (IOM, 2021), migrants' success in finding employment has typically been attributed to the skills and attributes they possess (e.g., Holmes and Marra, 2017), though more recently the responsibility of receiving countries to better support migrants (IOM, 2021) has been highlighted (see, for example, Greenbank and Marra, 2020 on refugees). Unlike prior (socio)linguistic research in this area, the current study concentrates on how economic migrants look for employment opportunities among their social group in diaspora. This, as explained later, responds to the natural cultural affinity between co-ethnics where language signals common origin and plays an important role in facilitating access to the London niche service economy where most Latin Americans are incorporated. This sector of the economy is characterised by informality and the activities performed therein are not always formally registered. Gaining access and sustaining employment opportunities relies on the establishment and maintenance of in-group relationships. These, in turn, ensure the economic viability of the social group.

2.1 Interconnectedness in a Diasporic Context: Beyond the Interpersonal Dyad

Social interaction between co-ethnics, in this case between Latin Americans and Spanish-speaking Latin Americans in particular, or other co-nationals in diasporic contexts such as the one this Element focuses on, is key to sustaining the livelihoods of the participants of this study and providing opportunities for economic betterment. As we will see in Section 4, the normative basis of social interactions among co-ethnics and the way relationships between members of the social group are constructed and assessed in diaspora are re-organised. This re-organisation responds, among others, to the social contacts migrants can

---

[3] Although see Fox and Jones (2013) for a critique of ethnicity and country of origin as key factors in explaining patterns of migration and settlement, especially in urban superdiverse (Vertovec, 2007) settings or in the case of 'pioneer migrants' (Bakewell et al., 2012). As suggested by the term, 'pioneer migrants' do not rely on an existing 'community' of culturally similar others. Instead, they draw on initial pre-existing social contacts with co-ethnics on arrival but move on to build networks of their own beyond co-ethnics or co-nationals by way of their cultural capital (Wessendorf, 2017).

avail themselves of to find their way in the receiving society, such as obtaining accommodation and employment. It also responds to how relationships with co-ethnics who offered direct or indirect assistance – quid pro quo transactions between two persons and transactions involving at least one third party (Molm, 2003), respectively – are maintained and the structural conditions of the receiving locales that migrants inhabit.

Some of the structural dimensions that the participants of this study inhabit entail the fact that migrants are differentially inserted into the labour market according to ethnicity (Wills et al., 2010), with Latin Americans in London generally occupying what is known as elementary employment positions in the segmented economy (e.g., cleaning and hospitality, see Section 3) (McIlwaine and Bunge, 2016). Access to national or local government resources (i.e., in the London Boroughs where they mostly live) depends on their legal status, that is, whether they are in a regular or irregular position,[4] and the extent to which the category of the population that sets them apart from the larger society and binds them together with similar others (i.e., Latin Americans) is recognised as an ethnic group locally or nationally. Indeed, recognition as an ethnic group is an essential requirement for accessing local government sources of funding. Time of arrival and length of settlement in the receiving society should also be borne in mind. The local sociopolitical circumstances in the receiving society at the time of arrival may preclude new or recent arrivals from accessing resources that other migrants may have had, such as free or accessible English language provision (Casey, 2016). Indeed, time of arrival, including entering the receiving country as a political refugee in the early 1990s,[5] coupled with length of settlement enabled some early arrivals to broker the labour market incorporation of those who arrived later (Márquez Reiter and Paz, 2013). Brokering is enabled by the social capital (Bourdieu, 1986), that is, the resources and

---

[4] Irregular migrants 'typically refers to migrants who are not entitled to reside in the receiving society, either because they never had a legal residence permit or because they have overstayed their time-limited permit' (Vollmer, 2011:2). The term, unlike others such as '(un) documented' migrants, seeks to capture the oscillating statuses that migrants often go through in the receiving society.

[5] In the early 1990s, asylum became a key political and policy issue in the United Kingdom as result of increased asylum applications during the 1980s and public concerns about levels of immigration. Prior to the 1993 Asylum and Immigration Appeals Act, asylum seekers were able to claim some cash benefits, had access to local authority housing, and, in some cases, were permitted to work (Dwyer and Brown, 2008). This is the case of late-1980s and early-1990s Latin American migrants who had access to free English language provision, often in local further education colleges. They studied English three times a week for circa nine hours, typically until First Certificate level (see britishcouncil.org), received assistance regarding housing as well as, in some cases, some discreet financial assistance to set up their own businesses (information gathered through ethnographic fieldwork from 2013 to 2015 comprising documentary evidence, non-participant observations, and interactions with first- and second-generation Latin American migrants as well as onward Latin American migrants).

advantages gained from the groups that early arrivals belong to and the people they know, as part of negotiating their lives with others in diaspora (Huschke, 2014). It is also enabled by the cultural capital (e.g., communicative competence in English) they may have gained since their own arrival in the receiving society, as well as the economic capital (Bourdieu, 1986) they may have accrued, such as owning their own cleaning company or commercial shops in Latin American enclaves which primarily cater for the needs of co-ethnics.

In this context of migration and diasporic life, therefore, the interconnectedness between migrants goes beyond the dyadic relationships that pragmatics has traditionally concentrated on or those it has more recently been attempting to grapple with as a result of evolving social media practices (see, for example, Garcés-Conejos Blitvich, 2022; Haugh, 2022; Jones, 2020; Lorenzo-Dus et al., 2011). The relational aspect of interactions between people has been part of the pragmatics agenda for a while, especially in (im)politeness research, where it has been seen to both affect and be affected by interactants' 'understandings of culture, society, and their own and other's "interpretations"' (Locher and Graham, 2010: 2). Of note in this area is Locher and Watts' (2008) discursive approach to relational work conceived of as 'all aspects of the work invested by individuals in the construction, maintenance, reproduction and transformation of interpersonal relationships among those engaged in social practice' (p.96). Also notable is Arundale's (2020) interactional approach to relating, understood as the establishment and maintenance of a connection between two otherwise separate individuals in interaction. These conceptualisations of relatedness, as well as others (e.g., Membership Categorisation Analysis, Fitzgerald and Housley, 2015), are principally based on the dyad and have focused on contexts where people's livelihoods are not at risk. They have been helpful in highlighting the importance of factors such as the background of the individuals involved in the exchanges examined and elements of the cultural context, especially when they surface and are made relevant in interaction. However, they have not considered the expectations of the wider participant base beyond reference to normativities of language in use based on middle-class milieus (cf. Bousfield, 2008) where language is often seen as a rather homogeneous system. Nor have they attempted to explicate why these factors emerged in the exchanges examined or contemplated the need to evidence them and ways to go about it.

In the setting examined here, the social networks in which language is embedded and are captured in the participants' accounts reveal that relationships within the social group are interlocked in a system of favours for primarily sustenance purposes. This interconnectedness cannot be detached from the structural dimensions which motivate it. The generally harsh lived experiences of the participants of this study – who often live on the margins of the larger society and suffer from substandard employment conditions – and the historical conditions that produce them are essential to comprehend the practice of occupational recommendations, even when these dimensions are not made relevant in the interview data. Only by considering the socio-economic and historical moment when the practice of work recommendations takes place, and its entanglement with the circumstances of the participants, can we reach a better understanding of the practice's raison d'être, its valorisation, and what this tells us about the participants' understandings of optimally appropriate relations within the wider participant base. This includes what their own role in these relationships is and how these roles become normative as guidelines for an ethical intra-diasporic life (Ames, 2021). The interconnectedness explored here thus inevitably involves the wider relational context in which the donor's (i.e., the recommender) and the beneficiary's (i.e., the recommendee) relationship is embedded as well as the place which it occupies within wider societal structures. The help that beneficiaries receive, especially though not limited to indirect assistance, has ramifications for the interpersonal relationship between the donor and the beneficiary but, importantly, it also bears on other relationships that either or both of the parties have within the social group (Márquez Reiter, 2022). Arguably, this is because Latin Americans in London continue to be segregated[6] despite their recently unprecedented victory against property development giants, the local council, and Transport for London in the now only Latin American enclave left in London.[7] Hence, they are reliant on intra-diasporic relations to make a living.

Against this background, the Element captures a snippet of a social environment in which the cultural, the situational, and the interpersonal dimensions that pragmatics has concentrated on (e.g., Senft, 2014) become unstable, as the creation of social bonds within the social group and the accountability that such relations ensue are primarily contingent on new socio-economic realities (Márquez Reiter, 2022). These socio-economic circumstances not only concern the donor and the beneficiary but other members of the social group too and principally underlie the participants' need for occupational mobility.

The conditions described here are not just experienced by the participants of this study, they constitute the present-day realities of thousands of people right on our doorsteps whose lives are embedded in inequalities. This requires a commitment to attend to the social and cultural elements of language in use (Verschueren, 2008), beyond academic or middle-class groups, with a view to raising awareness of communicative patterns previously

---

[6] www.theguardian.com/uk/2012/jun/22/london-latin-americans, accessed 1 July 2012.
[7] www.theguardian.com/commentisfree/2021/aug/19/tottenham-community-latin-village-new-way-to-regenerate, accessed 19 August 2021.

unexamined, test the aptness of our existing frameworks, and speak to current societal concerns. It is thus time for pragmatics to engage with some of the global challenges that have come to dominate the everyday lives of millions of people worldwide.

2.2 (Im)mobile Economic Migrants

As explained by Sheller and Urry (2006) when proposing the 'new mobilities' paradigm in the social sciences – a transdisciplinary paradigm which involves research from anthropology, cultural studies, geography, migration studies, science and technology studies, tourism and transport studies, and sociology – '[I]ssues of movement, of too little movement or too much, or of the wrong sort or at the wrong time, are central to many lives and many organisations' (p. 208). Despite this set of observable facts, social science was then rather static. Its objects of inquiries and the methodologies deployed to those ends were unable to capture and track the everyday reality of millions of people and institutions on the move, let alone entertain the notion that 'all mobilities entail specific often highly embedded and immobile infrastructures' (p. 208). In the case of the study reported in this Element, the occupational mobility that the participants often attain is emplaced within the segmented economy, usually within the co-ethnic niche economy, with few opportunities to move forward in the light of precarious work conditions (see Section 3).

Drawing on Sheller and Urry (2004, 2006), it could be claimed that despite recent advances in the social sciences, including those in the associated discipline of sociolinguistics, pragmatics appears to be 'a-mobile' (Sheller and Urry, 2006: 208) in terms of the language users it commonly focuses on or how it conceives of them. This, in turn, unwittingly leads pragmaticists to offer a picture of what is a primarily middle-class reality (Mills, 2017), a reality which is often skewed by the prominence and influence of studies on English. There seems to be a tendency in pragmatics to view language users as speakers of relatively stable languages (Vološinov, 1929/1973). Languages are often inadvertently presented as devoid of change (e.g., speakers of a given variety of a language) unless they are approached from a historical pragmatics angle (e.g., Culpeper and Kytö, 2000; Jucker and Taavitsainen, 2010), which, given the time scale involved, unavoidably moves the focus from language users to languages. These representations of languages and language users leave little room to account for the ordinariness of the heteroglossic practices (Bakhtin, 1981) which have been at the centre stage of sociolinguistic inquiry since the translanguaging turn (García, 2009; García and Li, 2014). Such hybrid communicative practices are, of course, not new and have received pragmatic attention (i.e., Gumperz' 1982 notion of inference).[8] The mobilisation of the communicative resources that language users have at their disposal[9] is, usually, explicated by shifts in language use. These changes are commonly accounted for by explanatory factors (e.g., gender, power, social class, etc.) which tend to be siloed[10] or accounted for by the situational context examined. The latter is usually idealised as rather uniform and harmonious (e.g., community of practice, Lave and Wenger, 1991) despite the peripheral practices which are often captured (see, for example, Dynel and Poppi, 2019 for an exception).

Research on some of the classic themes that have preoccupied pragmatics such as greetings and indirectness in the context of service encounters in two Latin American enclaves in London (Márquez Reiter, 2021) has reported the mobilisation and appropriation of linguistic indexicals (Silverstein, 2003) of dialects of Colombian Spanish which would have sounded alien in Colombia, especially for speakers of Bogotano Spanish – the 'prestigious' or 'educated' form of Spanish in Colombia. Put differently, it has captured the enregisterment (Agha, 2007) of forms of Spanish which in Colombia, especially in its capital city, are generally seen as less 'prestigious' for instrumental purpose. These transdialectal practices reveal the fluidity of language and communicative practices that users of given languages, in this case Colombian Spanish, can draw on and how they navigate them to engage in meaningful social interaction, in this case with co-nationals, with a view to obtaining assistance (e.g., employment, accommodation, etc.). Importantly, for the purposes of this Element, they demonstrate the sociopolitical and economic circumstances of making a living in London and help to explain economic migrants' reliance on co-ethnics, especially arrivals with relative social or economic capital, for occupational mobility purposes.

2.3 A Rationale for Examining Relatedness within Diasporic Groups

Migration and diaspora are classic topics of interest in sociology. As a group-focused discipline, sociology has examined various aspects of the migration process given that its patterns are typically conceived of as determinants of the

---

[8] Consider the famous 'gravy' example which was shown in the BBC documentary *Crosstalk* (1979), where a server of South Asian origin asks if gravy is wanted with the falling intonation most British and North American speakers of English, and presumably most Anglo Australians, New Zealanders, and South Africans too, associate with a statement instead of a question. The server's utterance, however, is interpreted by the clients as rude and perhaps even aggressive given that it is heard as performing a statement rather than it being an enquiry into the client's eating preferences.

[9] See, for example, Gumperz (1972/1986) on linguistic repertoires and Blommaert and Backus (2013) for an overview of repertoires in superdiversity.

[10] Some exceptions to this can be found in corpus studies which utilise parametric tests to measure the combination and impact of different independent variables on dependent ones.

size and rate of population growth as well as the structure and general characteristics of different populations. In other words, migration is often used as a lens from which to explore and understand social change in society. Some of the social phenomena that sociologists have examined include, but are not limited to, the effect of migrant remittances to the country of origin (e.g., Guarnizo and Portés, 1991), refugees and displaced people (e.g., Stepputat and Nyberg Sørensen, 2014), the dynamics of international labour migration (e.g., ILO, 2010), the relationship between citizenship and migration (e.g., Castles and Davidson, 2020), and the relationship between transnationalism and migration, whereby the former, broadly speaking, refers to the connections that migrants establish across countries taking into account those who are left behind (IOM, 2010) and transnational diasporic connections.

Similarly, various social theoretical models have attempted to explain patterns of occupational mobility in migratory contexts, such as the one examined in this Element. Of particular relevance are the economic theory of clubs and migrant network theory. The economic theory of clubs (see Dana, 2007 for an overview) provides a paradigm for the study of ethnic economies and ethnic entrepreneurship. It conceptualises the benefits derived from an ethnic grouping, such as accumulated social capital, decreased transaction costs, and the like, as a 'club' good which is supplied at the co-ethnic level, generally within an ethnic enclave, and with clear characteristics of excludability (Dana, 2007: 16). In the case of the participants of this study, this would apply to later arrivals, especially those with little cultural or social capital (Bourdieu, 1986).

Migrant network theory[11] posits that migrant networks entail interpersonal ties that help to connect migrants, in particular former migrants and non-migrants, both in origin and destination areas, through friendship, kinship, and a sense of common cultural origin. It is one of the theories that has been used to explain migration flows from members of a given cultural origin to a given destination area. It contends that migrants often follow the journey that other co-nationals have taken and that this, in turn, reduces the risks and costs of migration. Drawing on Bourdieu and Wacquant (1992), these connections can be seen as a form of social capital inasmuch as those who are part of the network can draw on them to gain access to foreign employment.[12]

Migrant network theory, however, does not address the relatively few, if any, contacts with social influence that economic migrants may have, such as the

---

[11] See Massey *et al.*(1993) for an overview of international migration theories.

[12] Social capital 'is the sum of the resources, actual or virtual, that accrue to an individual or a group by virtue of possessing a durable network of more or less institutionalised relationships of mutual acquaintance and recognition' (Bourdieu and Wacquant 1992: 119). Though see Coleman (1988) and Putnam (1995) for different understandings of social capital.

ones who participated in this study, or why members of the same network do not necessarily derive equal benefits (see, for example, Anthias, 2007). In addition, the theory tends to assume that new arrivals will access existing networks rather unproblematically (see, for example, White and Ryan, 2008 for a critique). In this sense, migrant network theory overlooks the interpersonal relations that are forged by migrants across time and space within the social group, including those that can be established or not given the constraints of the sector of the economy they occupy, among others.

Despite the synergies of the economic theory of clubs and migrant network theory with elements of the occupational recommendations analysed here, these theories do not explore or indeed attempt to approach an understanding of how non-elite migrants build or conceptualise interpersonal relations with others in diaspora, especially with co-ethnics and what the rules or normative expectations of such relations are. This is not to suggest that these theories have overlooked aspects of migration or migrant economies within the boundaries of their respective disciplines, let alone that they have no bearing on the analysis, but rather that their interest in these phenomena is different from those that this Element focuses on.

The socio-economic reality that the participants of this study face is one of mobility and immobility (Sheller and Urry, 2006) within their prerogative for economic betterment. This means that a new understanding of how relationality is enacted and sustained for occupational mobility purposes is required. The research reported in this Element, coupled with ongoing work with Latin Americans in London, confirms that most of the migrants I interacted with followed the journey of co-nationals who had migrated earlier. It also shows that these migrants, especially first-generation migrants, seek employment and other types of assistance through intra-ethnic contacts in diaspora, either prior to migration and/or on arrival. Importantly, the accounts provided by the Latin American participants highlight the importance of interpersonal connections and how these affect other relational connections within the social group. They offer us a window into how these social ties work. Such connections may involve knowing one or two people who may not necessarily form part of a social network such as a non-co-ethnic migrant who might be in a better position to provide assistance.

The present study does not address the validity of the various migration theories out there, as this is not its purpose. Instead, it uses them as backdrop from which to understand the relational nature of the social ties that the participants build and draw upon, primarily for instrumental purposes. This study seeks to shed light on the interpersonal pragmatics of the work recommendations that are reported to be performed by members of this social group in the London-based diaspora.

2.4 On the Connections between Work Recommendations and *Palanca*

The sociocultural practice of *palanca* has received attention in disciplines such as economics (e.g., Nitsch and Diebel, 2007) and intercultural communication (e.g., O'Rourke and Tuleja, 2009), mainly with a view to understanding cultural differences in business contexts within the formal economy. Indeed, *palanca* has been identified in the literature as an important element in the interdependency and interconnectedness with which Latin Americans are usually described relative to other cultures, particularly Western ones. An awareness of *palanca* has been posited as helpful for establishing business and work relations in Chile (Lomnitz,1971), Colombia (Archer and Fitch 1994; Fitch 1998), Mexico (García, 2016; Lindsley and Braithwaite, 2006; Lomnitz, 1977), and Peru (Ordoñez Bustamante and Sousa de Barbieri, 2003), where the practice is generally known as *argollas*.

Palanca is generally understood in the existing literature as comprising social networks or connections that have been built over the years, principally based on, though not limited to, the nuclear and extended family as well as with close ties. These connections enable those who are part of the network to procure favours such as employment positions or to gain access to scarce resources. However, the practice has not received attention in diasporic contexts. Migrants, especially economic migrants who work in the service sector, such as the participants of this study, must work incredibly hard to obtain economic mobility, and such mobility is rather limited. The dearth of studies of *palanca* in diasporic contexts could, potentially, be explained by the tendency to associate the practice with social circles of relative institutional influence and power and, the latter, with networks back home rather than in diaspora. Second, the very fact that economic migrants' main motivation for migrating is to obtain a better life abroad would, by default, mean that they have few *palancas* of relevant influence back home. For, if they had them, they would not need to migrate. Therefore, hearing that some migrants obtained sought-after elementary jobs by way of *palanca* was somewhat baffling to me.

In line with the literature on the subject, *palanca* represents a form of interpersonal connectedness through which positions or resources in the formal, rather than the informal, economy may be gained. In keeping with work recommendations, the interconnectedness that has been reported to underlie the practice of *palanca* makes possible the procuring of favours from those connections with political and/or economic influence. However, in the case of occupational recommendations, donors do not necessarily belong to influential social circles, and the positions they can procure for beneficiaries are typically characterised by precarity.

Many of the Latin American migrants I have interacted with have irregular status and are, naturally, reluctant to talk about the help and, often, the exploitation they have suffered at the hands of co-ethnics, among others. In a similar vein, those who enjoy a regular position do not tend to regard their achievements in London, such as obtaining a cleaning job, as a result of how *palanca* is conceived of in the literature. This, I argue, responds to the fact that members of this social group are principally employed in elementary positions in the service sector. Many of them work for less than the national living wage, have suffered downward mobility, and often articulate their employment status as being part of a servitude of services.

In addition, in order to keep their jobs or to progress within the service sector they have had to show their worth: hard-working individuals who are willing to be at a 24/7 disposal (see Section 4). Arguably, this would not be necessary if they had *palanca* back home or in London. What is more, *palanca* in their countries of origin is not necessarily about being hard-working or having the right skills for the jobs or general aspects of meritocracy. It entails having the right connections in the right places to open the door of opportunities, that is, having social capital (Bourdieu, 1986). It then follows that these opportunities do not necessarily have to be earned.

Given the limited resources that these migrants seem to have for a variety of reasons, such as insufficient understanding of how the UK works, how to navigate the system, lack of proficiency in English, access to affordable and accessible English language lessons, they are more dependent on co-ethnic contacts. Understanding the ways in which they relate to one another and (some of) the cultural rules governing their relations is important for gaining an insight into their everyday struggles for mobility, with wider ramifications for social and cultural inclusion and the role that pragmatics can play in an increasingly interconnected world.

The case study reported in this Element investigates the situated sociocultural practices which members of this social group report engaging in as they attempt to make a living in London by considering the wider relational context in which interpersonal relations are engrained and the structural conditions these migrants inhabit in their London localities.

The co-ethnic relationships that the participants of this study reflect on in their accounts highlight social bonds and feelings of diasporic belonging and membership, which are continually (re)negotiated. They reveal how interpersonal relations are unbound and shaped by the affective, socio-economic, and political situations that members experience (Brubaker, 2005; Márquez Reiter, 2022; Márquez Reiter and Patiño-Santos, 2021). It is against this background that the intelligibility and normativity of their behaviour often presents dilemmas that touch upon a newly reconfigured moral order (Márquez Reiter, 2022). The accounts examined in this Element are testament to the explicit normative discourses that emerge in such circumstances. The discourses that are constructed therein provide formulations of the norms that should govern appropriate behaviour among co-ethnics in the light of the conditioning environment they inhabit, coupled with the interpretative resources that are available to co-ethnic migrants by underlying cultural structures (Horgan, 2021:11). The latter allude to transcultural norms of behaviour and cultural coded elements of successful social performance (Alexander, 2004 in Horgan, 2021:11).

As the analysis of the accounts presented here will demonstrate (see Section 4), co-ethnics forge close interrelations with each other for principally instrumental purposes (i.e., occupational mobility). These relationships develop on different scales, ranging from interpersonal relationships within the wider social group in which they are emplaced to relationships with others back home in the light of diasporic relationships as well as person-to-person relationships. In this sense, therefore, the relationships reported here could be seen as translocal (see, for example, Appadurai, 1996) insofar as they simultaneously connect and influence different localities and people. In other words, the events which take place in one locality (i.e., back home or in diaspora) can influence either their locality or other connected places the participants of this study may have links to.

The types of relationships examined in this Element are best described as a form of exchange in terms of services and labour among co-ethnics who share a common interest: livelihood sustenance. Importantly, the relationships that are created and maintained by the participants of the study are, arguably, experienced by thousands of other migrants in London, elsewhere in the United Kingdom and beyond. Admittedly, they are likely to vary according to the different norms that are seen to regulate appropriate behaviour among different co-ethnic groups in the light of the conditioning environment they inhabit.

In the next section, the methods deployed to capture some of these migrants' sociocultural practices for occupational mobility in a local context, which is primarily constrained by immobility, will be presented.

3 Background and Methods

The subject of this Element was inspired by some of my lived experiences with Latin Americans in London for at least two decades, the experiences many fellow Latin Americans shared with me, and the reflective moment that finally inspired me to turn an academic lens to them. The analysis presented in

Section 4 is, however, primarily informed by interactions conducted over two years (2013–2015) in the most prominent Spanish-speaking Latin American enclaves in London and based on accounts gathered through ethnographically informed interviews with members of this social group. My lived experience and connections with Latin Americans in London and ongoing ethnographic work are, nonetheless, often used to add further context to the practices analysed, note the wider context in which they are situated (Márquez Reiter, 2021), and understand the contextual conditions that provided fertile ground for their emergence.

The selection of the two sites – Seven Sisters Indoor Market, Haringey and in and around the Elephant & Castle shopping centre, Southwark – corresponds to the relative high visibility of Spanish-speaking Latin Americans therein as exemplified by the number of shops, restaurants, and the like. The Elephant & Castle shopping centre was part of an urban regeneration project that has now seen Latin American and other retailers therein displaced as the shopping centre was demolished to make way for modern buildings that cater for London's insatiable housing needs. The Seven Sisters Market, on the other hand, won an unprecedented victory against property developers and Transport for London.[13] Notwithstanding this, Seven Sisters' path to gentrification is now felt in some of the market shops, especially eateries. Many of these have become a popular place for new locals living in the recently developed buildings in the area searching for a new culinary experience at reasonable prices, succumbing thus to the wafting smells of *bandeja paisa* and fresh *arepas* and consuming 'authentic' Colombian coffee.

Beyond their practical existence as markets, these enclaves are vital nexuses of knowledge and exchange; that is, they often constitute the first stop for Latin American migrants in London. They represent places to find guidance, support, and community.

I was a familiar face for many of the Latin Americans who worked in or visited these urban spaces at the time, in particular many of the retailers. Furthermore, my regular contact with Latin Americans in London as part of my own life as a Latin American living in the capital for over twenty years facilitated the data collection as various points of contacts had already been established and provided a good base from which to embark upon this project. This does not necessarily equate to the claim that my own life, or indeed my experience in London, more specifically, among Latin Americans in the capital would constitute the best starting point. My lived experience occurred at

---

[13] www.latinelephant.com, accessed on 9 January 2017, www.theguardian.com/uk-news/2021/aug/07/plans-for-190-flats-on-london-latin-village-site-scrapped-after-protests, accessed on 7 August 2021.

different times, locations, and scales, and I am what is generally referred to as a regular elite migrant rather than an (ir)regular economic migrant. In spite of having occupied similar employment positions as many of the participants of this study, my experience in the cleaning and hospitality sector was temporary and part-time and allowed me to pursue further higher-education qualifications – qualifications which were nonetheless needed given the structural dimensions that prevented me from converting my degrees into recognisable qualifications in the United Kingdom (e.g., reciprocity agreements between my country of origin and the United Kingdom).

3.1 Background

Almost 250,000 Latin Americans live in the United Kingdom with more than half of them in London (145,000), although this figure is likely to be higher given the irregular immigration status of some. Over a third of Latin Americans are Brazilian[14] followed by Colombians, who constitute the largest Spanish-speaking national group, with circa 30,000 members. This is followed by Ecuadorians, Argentineans, Venezuelans, and Mexicans (McIlwaine and Bunge, 2016).

Latin Americans – mainly Argentinean, Chilean, and Uruguayan nationals – arrived in the United Kingdom from the 1970s onwards, escaping their countries' dictatorships and political persecution. Some of these nationals helped to set up many of the associations that offer assistance to Latin American migrants and still form part of the London landscape today (e.g., Indoamerican Refugee Migrant Organisation, Casa Latinoamericana, etc.). Colombians and Ecuadorians constituted the majority of Latin American arrivals in the 1980s and 1990s, primarily motivated by political unrest in their own countries. The vast majority of Latin Americans in London arrived since 2000 for principally economic reasons (Márquez Reiter and Martín Rojo, 2015; McIlwaine et al., 2011). The economic crisis of 2008 resulted in onward migration of Latin Americans from mainland Europe, principally from Spain, thus increasing the diversity of the group as far as forms of Spanish are concerned and the ethnic mix. Onward migration has brought Cubans and Dominican nationals who are Afro descendants, among others, helping to diversify the landscape of these Latin American enclaves. This is especially visible on the weekends when these areas become a preferred rendezvous for relatively recent Spanish-speaking Latin American arrivals to socialise and relax.

---

[14] Brazilians are primarily concentrated in the Willesden Junction area of west London, where a high number of Brazilian-run businesses can be found. Many Brazilian shops and associations can also be found in Bayswater, Stockwell, and Vauxhall as well as in Elephant & Castle and Seven Sisters. In the last two areas Spanish-speaking Latin Americans figure prominently relative to Brazilians.

Latin Americans constitute the eighth largest non-UK-born population and the second fastest-growing migrant population in London (McIlwaine and Bunge, 2016), and Spanish is one of the top ten other languages spoken in the capital apart from English (Office for National Statistics, 2011). In line with many other migrant groups, Latin Americans have suffered significant downward occupational mobility as they are inserted differentially into destination labour markets according to a range of characteristics such as nationality, immigration status, race, gender, and language to create a 'migrant division of labour' (Wills et al., 2010). Despite the fact that half of Latin Americans have reported to be university educated, a quarter of them work in low-paid and low-skilled jobs, such as cleaning and hospitality. This figure rises to two-thirds in the case of onward Latin Americans (McIllwaine and Bunge, 2016). The lower position that most onward Latin Americans appear to occupy relative to first- or second-generation Latin Americans is arguably the result of their poorer contacts within the social group, in terms of the strength of the interpersonal ties and the social capital of their connections. Nevertheless, irrespective of their length of settlement, most of the Latin Americans in London have had some connection to cleaning or hospitality at some point in time. Thus, much in line with migration trends elsewhere, Latin Americans occupy a particular niche in the service sector of the labour market.

The analysis mainly focuses on interviews conducted with migrants who originally hailed from Colombia. This responds to the fact that they were one of the first Latin American national groups in the 1980s. At a time when UK immigration laws were not as constraining as they are today, they were able to benefit from free ESOL tuition as well as some financial assistance in terms of accommodation and economic integration (Márquez Reiter and Martín Rojo, 2015). This enabled first-generation Colombians, and, to a lesser extent, first-generation Ecuadorians too, to avail themselves of some of the business opportunities that other migrant groups provided them with as they attained further, albeit limited, mobility and integration. First-generation Colombians thus bought leases from shops previously owned by other migrants in socio-economically deprived multicultural shopping areas: the Elephant & Castle shopping centre and the Seven Sisters Indoor Market. At that time, some of these Colombian entrepreneurs[15] were

---

[15] A footprint of the regional origin of some of these early entrepreneurs, many of whom hailed from Antioquia and are known as *Paisas*, is present today in the menus of many Latin American eateries featuring *bandeja paisa* (a platter of red beans cooked with pork, white rice, minced meat, fried egg, plantain, black pudding, avocado, *chicharrón*, and *arepa*). This is also visible in the re-branding of the main bar and restaurant in the Seven Sisters Indoor Market (from *Parador Rojo* to *Pueblito Paisa*). At the time of writing this Element, the owners were a Colombian–Peruvian couple from Cali and Lima, respectively.

also able to buy the leasehold of many of the shops that formed part of these two commercial areas and rent them out to other co-nationals before selling them on. They also often run their own cleaning companies where they hire co-ethnics.

3.2 Data Collection

The fieldwork I carried out consisted of non-participant observations at the two largest enclaves of *Latinidad.* I visited the two shopping centres and surrounding areas on frequent occasions as a Latin American customer, albeit what some may regard as an 'elite' Latin American migrant by virtue of my occupation and physical appearance. My visits also took place on weekends when the sites were at their busiest. This entailed hanging around, observing, and taking notes of the activities that Latin Americans engaged in at the sites (i.e., watching what happens, listening to what is said, asking questions) as well as the general profile of those who regularly visit them by speaking to people informally, and identifying and interviewing key participants (i.e., major participants that the analyst relies on for validation of the data).

In these spaces I captured characteristic elements of Latin American cultural identity, principally though not exclusively, emblems of Colombianness as evidenced by the presence of national flags, images of tourist sites in the country, national dishes, and the like. The observations I conducted also captured the economic activity therein. Besides the consumption of food and drink, fieldwork revealed how these spaces can provide valuable information about the receiving society, especially for new arrivals or for those who do not feel confident enough in their ability to use English or have contacts who can help them to navigate the system. It also recorded instances of how the Latin Americans who were present therein related to one another, such as whether they visited the sites on their own, accompanied by others, how many others they seemed to know on arrival to the sites, and their general purpose for visiting. My observations of Latin Americans at the two sites were inevitably permeated by my own, albeit different, experience in London and my ongoing involvement with members of the social group. The observations made, informal questions asked, and documentary data gathered informed the life-story interviews (Atkinson, 1998). Table 1 illustrates the database from which the examples examined in this Element were taken.

Table 1 Database – fieldwork April 2013–September 2015

Observation diary – fieldnotes	Life-story interviews	Documentary evidence
12–15/4/2013 – *Parador Rojo*, Seven Sisters – file 1	Juan; Nélida; Luis Pedro; Lucía; Beatriz – 14/4/2013 Seven Sisters	*Latin News*; *Express News*: *El Ibérico*; *Voz Latina* – 4/2013–12/2014, digitised folder 1
13/5/2013 – *La Bodeguita*, Elephant & Castle – file 2	Patricia; Juan Carlos; Ana – 13/5/2013, Elephant & Castle	Flyers and offers – 4/2013–12/2014 – digitised folder 2
2/7/2013, 14/7/2013 – *Tiendas del Sur*, Elephant & Castle – files 2 and 3	Johan; Lucinda; Lourdes; Emma – 14/7/2013, Elephant & Castle	Photographs – folder 3
8/9/2013, 22/9/2013 – *La Juguería*, Seven Sisters – file 4	Blankita; Pablo; Ana; Pocha – 21/9/2013, Seven Sisters	
15/11/2013, 16/11/2013 – *Asesoría Legal*, Seven Sisters – file 5	Carmelita; Amparo; Walter, María; Antonio – 14/11/2013, Seven Sisters	
4/2/2014, 5/2/2014 – *The Arches*, Elephant & Castle – file 6	Rico Pato; Fernando; Rosana – 5/2/2014, Elephant &Castle	
16/4/2014, 17/4/2014 – *Carnicería de María*, Seven Sisters – file 7	Doña María y marido; Susana (2) – 17/4/2014, Seven Sisters	
20/7/2014 – *Costurería*, Elephant & Castle – file 8	Cristina; clienta –20/7/2014, Elephant & Castle	

3/9/2014, 4/9/2014 – *Peluquería*, Seven Sisters – file 9

Patricia; Liliana – 5/9/2014, Seven Sisters

24/12/2014 – *Fiesta de Navidad*, Seven Sisters – file 10

Abuelitas (2) – 24/12/2014, Seven Sisters

2/2/2015, 4/2/2015 – *Fajas*, Seven Sisters – file 11

Catalina – 3/2/2015, Seven Sisters

30/4/2015– *Tienda de re-mix*, Elephant & Castle – file 12

Clientes (2) – 30/4/2015, Elephant & Castle

3/7/2015– *Lo del Tigre*, Seven Sisters – file 13

Darío – 27/5/2015

22/12/2015, 23/12/2015 – *Money exchange*, Seven Sisters – file 14

Dueño; Julio – 23/12/2015

Systematic non-participant observations were carried out over a two-year period (2013–2015). A total of approximately thirty hours of observations (Spradley, 1980) were conducted during peak and slow hours in the shops in and around the Elephant & Castle shopping centre and Seven Sisters Market. It was while conducting descriptive observations (Spradley, 1980) of service encounters between Latin American providers and customers in the above areas that I witnessed how Latin American recent arrivals often approach the counters of (coffee) shops and restaurants in pursuit of potential work opportunities. Herein is an example of two such cases taken from fieldnotes. The content of the interactions was recalled and written down post event, relying thus on my memory and interpretation of what took place aided by the prompts that were scribbled in situ.

10/10/2013 Seven Sisters – Parador Latino [field notes]

Mid-morning while I'm ordering a coffee at *El Parador Latino*,[16] a middle-aged Colombian woman approaches the counter and waits until the attendant serves me the coffee:

Woman:	*Qu'hubo?*
	Hello
Attendant:	*mm*
Woman:	*me regalas un minutico?*
	Do you have a minute to talk?
Attendant:	*Qué pena señora pero estamos trabajando. Qué necesita?*
	I'm sorry M'am but we're working. What do you need?
Woman:	*mire estoy buscando trabajando. Necesitan a alguien en la cocina o dónde sea?*
	Look I'm looking for work. Do you need anyone in the kitchen or anywhere?
Attendant:	*pues creo que no pero tiene que hablar con el dueño*
	I don't think so but you need to talk to the owner
Woman:	*a qué hora lo encuentro?*
	At what time can I find him?
Attendant:	*pues no sé pase dentro de un hora si quiere, capáz que tiene suerte*
	I don't know but pop by in half an hour if you like, you may find him then

3/03/2015 Elephant & Castle – music shop [fieldnotes]

---

[16] The name of the coffee shop is fictitious.

While talking to the owner of a music shop in Elephant & Castle specialising in burning bespoke Latin tunes, a man in his twenties comes in and addresses the owner:

Man: *Muy buenas tardes. Estoy buscando a Don Eduardo*
           Good afternoon. I'm looking for Mr Eduardo

Owner: *Habla con el mismo*
           You're talking to him

Man: *Don Eduardo mucho gusto, señora disculpe la molestia*
           Mr Eduardo pleased to meet you, M'am sorry for the inconvenience

Me: *No, no hay problema*
           No, no problem

Man: *Me ha dicho el señor de la carnicería, Don Luis, que pueda que usted necesite quien le pueda dar una mano aquí*
           Don Luis the butcher told me that you might need someone to give you a hand here

Owner: *Don Luis? De qué carnicería?*
           Don Luis? From which butchers?

Man: *De Las Dos Arenas en Brixton*
           From Las Dos Arenas in Brixton

Owner: *Ah sí, pero qué pena con usted pero no, no necesitamos a nadie*
           Ah yes but I'm sorry but no, we don't need anyone

The man thanks the owner as he leaves the shop. Once he is outside the shop, the owner looks at me and says:

Owner: *Yo no sé ni de quién me habla. A mí Luis, si es que es el Luis que yo conozco, no me dijo nada.*
           I don't even know who he referred to. Luis, if it is the Luis I know, didn't mention anything to me.

The content of these observations highlights the importance that is attributed to contacts and that recommendations from the right contacts provide a better chance of getting a foot in the door. These observations coincide with the views informally expressed by Latin Americans during the various interactions with me as epitomised in the expression *el que tiene padrino no muere infiel* (Literally: 'if you have a godfather you don't die as an infidel', idiomatically: 'It's not what you know but who you know'). As analysts, however, we should thoughtfully examine the assessments made by participants and not take them at face value (see, for example, Goebel, 2015), especially as work recommendations, not only require 'who you know' but 'what you know'; and, importantly knowing that what you know should not always be disclosed.

In view of the foregoing, a long-term ethnographic project in which members of this social group working in a particular segment of the economy were shadowed and recorded throughout their daily lives would have offered a prime lens through which to examine work recommendations in action. However, the very nature of the situated sociocultural practice under study in certain segments of the economy, such as the unregulated economy, to name one, would entail significantly adverse ethical considerations, including issues of health and safety for the researcher and others involved (see, for example, Fielding, 1981). The risk of harm was thus considered in relation to the potential benefits of conducting ethnographic research in the workplace. Part and parcel of conducting ethnographic research entails the achievement of trust between the different parties involved in the process. It then follows that in certain spheres of unregulated trading practices, the researcher would most likely not be granted access unless they were a willing participant. Given these ethical considerations, documentary material and ethnographic information, that is, observations and interactions with members of the Latin American social group, were used to inform the interviews.

3.3 Interviews

Based on the contacts gained through ongoing fieldwork in the Latin American community, thirty-eight life-story interviews (Atkinson, 1998) were conducted at the Seven Sisters Indoor Market and the Elephant & Castle shopping centre. The average length of each interview was forty minutes. These resulted in circa thirty-five hours of recordings that were later transcribed, anonymised, and uploaded to NVivo 11 to organise the data, classify segments of the interviews into themes (Braun and Clarke, 2006), link them to research notes, and carry out search-and-retrieve operations to aid the examination of possible relationships between the themes. Thematic categories were identified 'through researcher interpretation, rather than being strictly determined in advance' (Paulus and Wise, 2019:162). The main themes were: the basis of a recommendation, confidence in the beneficiary's work ethics and moral character, and Colombians work well. NVivo was mainly used as a data management tool to visualise and search the database in its entirety. It facilitated the identification of sub-categories or themes according to their recurrence in the interviews and in line with the profile of the participants (first- or second generation, country of origin, time of arrival, length of settlement).

I first approached those I was familiar with and quickly obtained a referral from these participants to others. The snowball technique (O'Reilly, 2009) used to recruit interview participants was deemed the most appropriate method for sampling given the centrality of networking, the referral it entails, and their importance for this study. I thus started with a small number of initial contacts and invited them to become participants. The agreeable participants were then asked to recommend other contacts who potentially might also be willing participants, who then, in turn, recommended other potential participants, and so on. I, therefore, used my own social networks to establish initial links, with sampling momentum developing from these. This allowed me to capture an increasing chain of participants. While snowballing increases the number of participants, as people become more receptive to the researcher when the latter has been vouched for by a member of the social group as trustworthy, the participants are more likely to know one another in some way or other (Lincoln and Guba, 1985). That is, they are likely to be part of some sort of a social network. In the two settings examined, however, contact between Latin Americans is ubiquitous and the main raison d'être. These contact spaces potentially offer alternative labour market possibilities that do not demand the same requirements of the receiving society: they eliminate language barriers, and, as we will see in Section 4, they can be used to circumvent other requirements such as the need to be in a regular position to find employment. That the bulk of participants of this study hailed from Colombia is thus not surprising for they constitute the majority of Spanish-speaking Latin Americans in London, and most of the shops at the time when the observations and interviews were carried out were run by Colombians.

The life-story interviews were conducted in situ as the participants worked in the two sites. They were thus carried out in a public space. The fact that some of the participants who were subsequently interviewed overheard part of the interviews acted as reassurance that nothing sinister would happen to them through their participation. Before conducting the interviews, consent was sought by informing potential participants of the purposes and procedures of the research, the risks and benefits associated with the study, and how the data provided by them would be protected and stored.[17]

Life-story interviews constitute open interviews in which participants are asked to share their life story with the interviewer. In the case of this study, participants were asked about their migratory experiences and how they obtained employment in London. This enabled me to gain an understanding of how their accounts speak to both micro- and macro-level issues of their diasporic experience. That is, they allow the examination of how local, group-based, and societal changes are understood and responded to within 'ordinary' lives (Roberts, 2014). By inviting participants to look back on their journeys to obtaining employment in London, their experiences and how they interpret them, the way in which they understand the world around them can be gained (Faraday and Plummer, 1979). Life-story interviews constitute an important vehicle for studying groups of people whose lives have been almost

---

[17] The study received a favourable ethics approval from my previous academic institution.

invisible in official discourse (Chamberlayne et al., 2000). They represent a useful tool for examining the participants' incorporation into the niche and principally informal service economy of which information is largely absent in official and academic discourse. Furthermore, life-story interviews provide 'considerable background and social texture' (Berg, 2007: 277) to how relationships among social groups are established and sustained.

Through these interviews, the participants provided accounts of their migration trajectory and their incorporation into the labour market in their own words, recounting, and reflecting on, events in their own lives without too much intervention from the researcher in terms of predetermined questions. The interviewees thus talked about their experiences, often relating them to other life events, and in this process, they offered evaluations of their normative expectations. The accounts we examine here are indicative of a dialogical relationship between differentially situated participants (Yuval-Davis, 2013): the interviewer, the interviewee, and those whose stories emerged in the interviews. In addition, these accounts are often conditional on the way in which the prompts are delivered and designed by the interviewer (Márquez Reiter, 2018).

Despite the unstructured format that life-story interviews can take, the core guiding questions revolved around the participants' contacts prior to migrating and on arrival, as these were observed to be relevant to securing employment within the co-ethnic niche market. These entailed: the kind of relationship the participants had with these contacts, their assessment of the help they received from them, including the type of bond that was thus re-established, the type of favours that are deemed appropriate in these circumstances, the reciprocity that they accrue, if any, and its connection to *palanca* where appropriate (see Example 13).

I sometimes found that staff at the front of the shops and its clientele had changed, primarily owing to the constant transformation of urban centres (Vertovec, 2007) and onward migration of Latin Americans from Spain. This resulted in a change of front-desk service providers from 1990s Latin American migrants to post-2008 migrants, mainly Spanish passport holders. In these situations, I used personal recommendations from my network of Latin American connections to maximise the chances of recruiting voluntary participants. This helped me to approach new faces by way of a personal recommendation. It decreased the natural level of suspicion and mistrust of having an unknown person asking relatively private questions such as their journey to the United Kingdom, how they had obtained employment, accommodation, and other forms of general assistance, especially in cases when the participants' immigration status or that of the person who assisted them was not entirely clear.

In 2013, a relatively large number of onward Latin American migrants arrived in London (22,000 arrivals compared to 44,000 already in the United Kingdom; McIlwaine and Bunge, 2016). Prior to Brexit, onward Latin American migrants met the legal conditions for entry and settlement. In spite of this, making a living in London has also been challenging for them (Márquez Reiter and Patiño-Santos, 2021). In keeping with first-generation Latin Americans and many second-generation Latin Americans, onward Latin American migrants are also largely inserted in the service industry (e.g., in the cleaning and hospitality sectors) under precarious conditions (zero-hour contracts, minimum wage or below; Berg, 2019). In common with many first-generation Latin Americans, onward Latin Americans migrants have also suffered deskilling (Baum, 2015; McIlwaine and Bunge, 2019) and do not have sufficient knowledge of English that is, they do not feel confident enough in using it or, for that matter, have not had opportunities to formally learn the language.

The year 2020 marked a historical moment in the United Kingdom as the country left the European Union. The effects of Brexit are palpable across the country; however, these are mainly tangible in the regulated economy rather than in the niche segment of the economy where most Latin Americans – first-, second-generation, and onward migrants – and those who participated in this study are mainly incorporated. Although London is the region of the United Kingdom in which EU migrants make up the highest share of the population, in 2020 roughly 7 per cent of people employed in the United Kingdom were EU born, with a sharp decline in EU migration (42%) in the post-Brexit referendum period from countries such as Spain.[18]

In this sense, therefore, the geographical mobility of Latin Americans coming from European destinations has decreased substantially, but the socio-economic mobility of Latin Americans with European and British citizenship appears to remain roughly similar. The fall in the value of the sterling pound which reduced the value of money earned in the United Kingdom compared to other EU countries and the political uncertainty brought about by Brexit, among others, has led to significantly fewer onward migrants. However, ongoing engagement with fellow Latin Americans in London, including those who arrived as onward migrants, indicates that the latest arrivals continue to search for employment among the social group. For many of these posts, their legal status is not necessarily a sine qua non for employment.

3.4 Data Analysis

The accounts gathered through the interviews are conceived of as reflective perceptions of relatedness insofar as they make manifest the perceived norms

---

[18] Sumption and Walsh (2022) www.migrationobservatory.ox.ac.uk/wp-content/uploads/2019/07/MigObs-Briefing-Migrants-in-the-UK-labour-market-an-overview.pdf. Available data refer to EU citizens as EU born. Onward Latin American migrants with EU citizenship typically obtain EU status after a period of settlement in Europe.

that (ought to) bind members of the group together and those they understand as relevant in their interactions with me (i.e., a researcher of Latin American origin). They thus represent participants' metapragmatic judgements of the appropriateness or lack of appropriateness of the behaviour of members of the social group, including their own (Culpeper and Haugh, 2021; Hyland, 2017). They constitute instances of language use that have aspects of normative behaviour as their reflexive object (Verschueren, 2021). In other words, they reveal what the participants conceive of as optimally appropriate relations within the social group, that is, their metapragmatic understanding of the moral order of the social group and their place therein. The discursive analysis of the metapragmatic evaluations present in the interview accounts considers how they are constructed and speak to the socio-economic realities that the participants live in.

Interviews constitute a useful lens from which to explore perceptions of behaviours and relevant rationalisations of normative expectations, in this case, those regarding the construction and maintenance of relationships within the social group for primarily sustenance purposes. Interviews can be a locus for the emergence of ideologies (Márquez Reiter, 2018). They have an ideological dimension for they enable evaluations about what ought to be, both in terms for they enable evaluations of what ought to be, both in terms of how they are constructed in situ, that is, as part of the positions (role-identities) and stances (points of view) the participants adopt throughout the encounter, and those that circulate in the larger community and are invoked or reproduced therein (Wortham et al., 2011). The examination of these essentially metapragmatic judgements is not siloed. They are supplemented with an understanding of the point of view from which they are articulated. Crucially, the ethnographic observations and documentary evidence gathered allow us to make sense of how the reflective moments represented by the accounts align with the historical and socio-economic realities that the participants face, whether these are discursively invoked or made relevant in micro moments of the life-story interview as a situated interaction in and of itself (Briggs, 1986; De Fina and Perrino, 2011).

Central to the analysis I present here is that different researchers may indeed report different 'realities' and display different levels of self-awareness. The fieldwork I conducted could be described as embodied and often carried out discomfort. This embodiment responds to the fact that I am Latin American and that I can speak the 'language' fluently as the questions I asked the participants (see Section 3.3) are based on aspects of my own lived experience and those that have been shared with me over the years. While I did not disclose my own experiences in the cleaning sector, the tacit affinity I had with the participants meant that my questions were rarely resisted. They were based on my epistemic reflexivity and reacted to as making sense of the participants' lived experiences which, by and large, they were comfortable to share with me. However, they often constituted uncomfortable listening for me owing to my own assessments based on the position I occupy in this social space (Wacquant, 1989). This is a position that as an individual, though not necessarily as a researcher, I embody (Bourdieu, 2007). It is a social space that I, unlike them, could come in and out of, but one that troubled me given my inability to navigate my own individual/researcher duality to act on some of the injustices observed. To put it in another way, listening to the struggles of the participants and how they wrestle with the conditions of a diasporic life in London brought to bear introspection on my epistemic reflexivity (Maton, 2003) as an individual and as a researcher. It constituted a double form of reflexivity (Verschueren, 2021).

4 Analysis: Towards an Understanding of Occupational Recommendations

Leveraging connections to obtain employment is a process. However, the personal and often intimate nature of the interpersonal relationships that are leveraged for instrumental purposes represents a methodological challenge for capturing and tracking the practice in action. The accounts obtained in the interviews offer us a lens to examine some of the participants' own reflexive understandings of their sociocultural practices, with special attention to those they engage with to sustain their livelihoods in London. Admittedly, they provide us with an approximation of the phenomena under study, revealing some of the complex relationships of experiences across time and space (back home and in diaspora) as recalled by members from this group. The participants reflect on the practice by articulating aspects of the process and evaluating the actions that led to a given state of affairs. Through these evaluations, the participants (implicitly) sanction or condone certain behaviours as being out of line or falling short of behavioural expectations. In other words, they retrospectively articulate evaluations of the actions that have or ought to have taken place (see Culpeper, 2011; Kádár and Márquez Reiter, 2015; Márquez Reiter, 2022; Márquez Reiter and Kádár, 2022). In so doing, they shine a light on normative behavioural expectations regarding interpersonal relations, issues of (im)mobility, especially occupational mobility, and their own trajectory in diaspora.

The meta-commentary embedded in these accounts also allows us to capture some of the participants' aspirations as to how things should be, particularly the behavioural norms that should be attended to by members of their social group. In other words, how optimally appropriate relations are understood by members of the group and how the roles of individuals in diasporic work relationships become guidelines for an ethical life (Ames, 2021). Social norms are understood here as actions which are regarded by members of this social group as appropriate (Bendor and Swistak, 2001). They represent socially enforceable expectations as to what constitutes appropriate actions (Coleman, 1990) in the London-based Spanish-speaking Latin American diaspora. They are supported by the expectation that their non-adherence will be sanctioned (Bendor and Mookherjee, 1990), especially when the labour chain that maintains the primarily economic order on which the livelihood of the group rests is upset. As the analysis will show, the norms that the participants invoke in their accounts have been developed in the light of the structural conditions the participants inhabit and the limited agency, broadly conceived of as the ability or willingness to act (Laidlaw, 2010), this provides them with.

The following section thus examines the practices that the participants report engaging in with their first- or second-order contacts (relatives and close friends vs. acquaintances) in pursuit of mobility, such as obtaining employment, accommodation, and access to services.

4.1 Personal Recommendations

One of the ways in which obtaining employment is reported among Latin Americans in London is via recommendations through personal contacts. This is hardly surprising in the light of the fact that the migrants often follow in the footsteps of those who migrated earlier owing to the (potential) advantages that such connections may bring, and that many of them, especially new arrivals, are not communicatively competent in English.

As mentioned earlier, Latin Americans in London are largely inserted into the co-ethnic labour market which is generally unregulated. This typically entails working in a cleaning company or restaurant run by co-ethnics or in similar service sector jobs where the supervisor is a co-ethnic and the jobseeker does not have to deal with customers directly or communicate with non-co-ethnic workers to perform their tasks. In these cases, therefore, knowledge of English is not, strictly speaking, necessary for incorporation into the niche labour market. The supervisor is often bilingual and acts as an intermediary between the workers and the management (see, for example, Goldstein, 1997).

Although communicative competence in English does not play a significant role in preventing access to the informal economy (Vigouroux, 2013), it is conceived of as a *sine qua non* for improving job prospects. It lessens the dependency on Latin American personal connections and offers the possibility of establishing contacts outside the co-ethnic group in London. In addition, job prospects are likely to improve if the jobseeker has regular status. In those cases where the jobseekers are regular migrants with some knowledge of English, as is the case of some post-2008 arrivals with European passports, principally from

Spain, the chances of obtaining a job behind the counter in Latin American shops or serving in restaurants, rather than cleaning, were, prior to Brexit, increased. While this may be seen as offering more social status among co-ethnics, it does not necessarily translate into better economic returns.

The faces at the front of many of the shops in the two commercial clusters where the data were collected had changed since the arrival of onward Latin American migrants from Europe. Prior to this, business owners, typically 1980s and 1990s arrivals, were often seen behind the counters of their shops, accompanied by fellow Latin American staff. Shop owners often expressed the difficulties they encountered in finding staff with regular status that they could trust to stay in the job, who also had some knowledge of English and could therefore work at the interface with non-Latin American clients. The arrival of onward migrants resolved the regular status issue and the relative permanence of these workers in the job.[19] It provided owners with a new pool of applicants for these positions at a time when the business clusters were transformed by the presence of onward Latin American migrants who regularly visited these spaces in search of jobs, assistance, and the establishment of connections. It also allowed many owners to free up some of their time to concentrate on other ventures or simply to get some respite from habitually long working days.

4.2 The Basis of a Recommendation

According to the participants interviewed, and in line with the observations conducted as well as my own experience among Latin American friends in London, recommendations are effected when the recommender suggests to a personal contact within the group that the recommendee would be a 'good worker'. A recommendation thus constitutes a directive speech event (Austin, 1961): the recommender aims to get a third party (one of their relational contacts) to employ the recommendee or to find someone within their connections to find them employment. In the unfolding analyses, we will see that certain conditions need to be met to effect a recommendation and why these are important to maintain the economic order.

The recommender may not necessarily be aware of any positions available but may, nonetheless, put the recommendee in contact with one of their

---

[19] Staff working for ethnic businesses typically earned the minimum wage (£7.50 per hour- April 2017–March 2018) compared to private and, often undeclared, household cleaning jobs in London, where the rates oscillated between £10 and £12 per hour. A few of the early onward Latin American migrants, especially those with dependents, have been able to receive some financial support from their local councils, such as assistance with their rent, provided their earnings were below a given threshold (www.gov.uk/housing-benefit/what-youll-get). This, in turn, would make a part-time minimum wage job at an ethnic shop more financially manageable.

horizontal connections who may, in turn, have relevant information on potential sources of employment or other forms of assistance, such as accommodation. Connecting recommendees to people they are unfamiliar with can potentially expand the sources of information about where work can be found and offer a chance for recommendees to enlarge their contacts within the social group.

In Example 1, Lucía, a hairdresser from Colombia who had been living in Spain for over eighteen years prior to migrating to London in 2008, explains that friends in London from her native Medellín encouraged and facilitated her onward migration to the capital. They knew of an opening at a salon where she still worked when interviewed.

EXAMPLE 1. LUCÍA – ONWARD MIGRANT [INTERVIEW 7]

The interviewer is identified as R throughout the transcripts, whereas the interviewees are identified by the initial of their fictitious first name. Throughout the Element, examples are offered in the original language with their corresponding translations into English in the Appendix. This represents a small step towards ensuring that data in languages other than English are given their rightful place in sociopragmatic research.

58	R:	Y las amigas de dónde las conocías de Medellín?
59	L:	De::(h) de Colombia sí
60	R:	De Colombia mismo (.) y::m:: y sigues en contacto
61		con ellas?
62	L:	Sí:=
63	R:	=Viven aquí ta=
64	L:	=ajá=
65	R:	=okey (.)Y: tú has necesitado ayuda para ir al mé:dico
66		al denti:sta=
67	L:	=a:::(h) (ahí) siempre claro (.) imagínese si no
68		hablamos inglés
69	R:	Y quién te prestaba su ayuda
70	L:	Bueno todo el mundo (0.3) cuando uno llega aquí:(h)m
71		(.) .hh a ver quién me puede acompañar aquí ()
72		uno le recomienda al uno el otro al otro (y uno) ya a
73		mí me han acompañado .HH (.) tantas personas que ya ni
74		me acuerdo cuántas (.) para todas las cosas que uno
75		tiene que hacer cuando llegas

In keeping with the views (implicitly) expressed by all the participants (38/38) in the interviews conducted, and with the literature on migration studies (e.g., Granovetter, 1995; de Haas et al., 2020), contacts in the country of destination facilitate the migration journey. In most cases, they ensure the arrival's initial welcome by providing a temporary roof over their heads or, in some cases such as Lucía's, a job servicing the needs of the Latin American "community" too (i.e., working at a salon whose clientele is primarily Latin American). Upon learning earlier in the interview that Lucía had been in London for over seven years working at the same salon, is fully immersed in the Latin American group, and based on knowledge gained from ongoing ethnographic work and my involvement with members of the group, I asked her if she needed help to seek medical assistance. My question at l. 65 (*Y: tú has necesitado ayuda para ir al mé:dico al denti:sta*, 'and: have you needed help to see a doctor or a dentist') conveyed the presupposition (e.g., Levinson, 1983) that Lucía was not communicatively competent in English. My presupposition was immediately validated by Lucía's direct answer (*a:::(h) (ahí) siempre claro* 'u:::((h) (there) always of course' l. 67) and the account that subsequently followed (*imagínese si no hablamos inglés* 'imagine if we don't speak English').With this account, Lucía elaborated on her confirmation. She presented herself as part of the Latin American collective as observed in the use of the first-person plural *hablamos* ('we speak'). The Latin American collective is categorised as bereft of the necessary language skills for its members to enact agency (Laidlaw, 2010), lessen their dependency on co-ethnic contacts, and achieve (further) mobility. Her account, however, contradicts her validation of my question at l. 65. If she has received help to attend to her medical needs but does not speak English, someone who speaks English and has at least some competence in Spanish must have helped her. It would then follow that not everyone in the social group is monolingual.

The categorisation of Latin Americans in London as monoglots is one of the various discourses that circulate among members of the social group (Márquez Reiter, 2018). Indeed, English is often reported as one of the main obstacles towards attaining mobility (Márquez Reiter and Martín Rojo, 2015; McIllwaine and Bunge, 2016) and as an essential requirement for social inclusion (APPG, 2017). The situation on the ground is, however, more complex. Eighties and nineties arrivals usually speak English given that at that time ESOL provision was free of charge and migrants often attended (evening) courses at their local further education colleges. In addition, many 1.5-generation Latin Americans and second-generation Latin Americans are generally bilingual. They have been secondarily socialised in the receiving society. As mentioned earlier (in Section 3), as analysts we should closely examine the assessments made by participants rather than simply accept them as 'truths' even when they are made relevant in the data. Understanding the contextual conditions where the lives of the participants are embedded is essential to make sense of the claims made.

In view of this, I asked Lucía a specifying question (Thompson et al., 2015, l. 69 *y quién te prestaba su ayuda*, 'and who helped you'). Lucía responded with a generalisation in which she invoked the solidarity that allegedly exists between Latin Americans (*me han acompañado .HH (.) tantas personas que ya ni me acuerdo cuántas*, 'I've been accompanied by so many people that I cannot remember how many' l. 73–4) on arrival (*para todas las cosas que uno tiene que hacer cuando llegas* 'for all the things one has to do when you arrive' l. 74–5). In her response (l. 70–5) she describes the practices new arrivals engage in: ask for help from those whom you know to establish if they, in turn, know of anyone in their network that might be able to help. Lucía thus shines some light on how recommendations can be effected within the social group.

Lucía's relatively successful onward journey from Spain to London does not coincide with that of many post-2008 arrivals who, despite having a contact with whom to stay on arrival, encountered various difficulties finding their bearings within the Latin American group. Patricia's account, in Example 2, illustrates some of the tensions that exist between early arrivals and onward Latin American migrants (Márquez Reiter and Patiño-Santos, 2017; Patiño-Santos and Márquez Reiter, 2019). Embedded in Patricia's account is an example of the lack of solidarity that she has experienced from fellow Latin American migrants and its connection to her migration trajectory (i.e., an onward migrant from Spain). Patricia's experience thus stands in stark contrast with that reported by Lucía. Example 2 starts with Patricia's assessment of the way early arrivals treat onward migrants in response to my question of whether she had received help from more established members of the social group.

EXAMPLE 2. PATRICIA – ONWARD MIGRANT [INTERVIEW 24]

80 P: Entonces discriminan mucho la gente que viene ya y
81   como llegamos de últimos entonces te tienen un poquito
82   de ventaja ya nos quieren:(h) o sea sacarnos
83   a nosotros porque nos: si va uno a pedir un favor
84   sí yo te lo hago pero te cobro tanto .HH por una
85   simple llamada (.) que es (hasta) inhu- inhumano que
86   cobren una llamada entre compañeros que estamos fuera
87   de nuestras tierras y .HH [pero bueno es la vida]
88 R: [pero son colombianos] que
89   han estado aquí toda la vida=
90 P: =que han estado aquí toda la vida sí que llevan
91   cuarenta treinta y cinco años
92 R: Sí sí yo sé
93 P: Pero desgraciadamente es así a mí eso me me me me
94   me fastidia un montón porque mira yo digo vamos a ver
95   si estamos todos en la misma lucha todos queremos
96   salir .hh por qué hacemos eso? por qué no podemos
97   echar una manit si no cuesta nada una llamada si
98   es de mi mismo teléfono (.) pero te cobran entonces
99   ya: pa mi eso me descompone un montón sabe? .HH

Patricia had been in London for three years when the interview was conducted. Her account indicates that it is not sufficient to have contacts in London but that it is necessary to have quality contacts, that is, connections that can effect help from others. In keeping with the stories from other migrants (30 out of 38), and those with links to Latin Americans in London, Patricia being charged for menial interpreting jobs such as making a call or booking an appointment in English (l. 84–5), despite using her own telephone and thus paying for the call herself, is not a rare occurrence. Other tasks, which at first sight may be interpreted as costly by newly arrived migrants, such as procuring a school admission for a child in a state school, are free of cost and managed by the relevant local council. In spite of this, so-called legal advisers charge a fee for completing the relevant forms in English and submitting them to the council.

Despite the normalcy with which the practice of charging co-ethnics for low-cost tasks (Brown and Levinson, 1987) is articulated by various shop owners and its observed pervasiveness, especially by onward migrants and post-2000 arrivals with limited knowledge of English and relevant contacts in the social group, Patricia evaluates the practice as immoral. The material gains that underlie Patricia's description of relationships with co-ethnics go against the basic value of solidarity that, in her view, should bind Latin American migrants together in view of their common struggles for mobility. However, sustaining a livelihood in London can be challenging for all. As previously mentioned, Latin Americans primarily rely on each other to make a living, and new arrivals create a demand for services which, owing to limited (local) governmental support (e.g., interpreting services), are provided by those with a longer duration of settlement in return for some financial remuneration.

This begs the question of who meets the requirements to receive help from others or to be put in touch with the recommender's contacts. In Example 3, Pablo, a 1990s migrant from the Vallecaucano in Colombia, who now owns a Latin American eatery, explains that the practice of connecting co-ethnic migrants in search of employment with fellow migrants is common practice.

EXAMPLE 3. PABLO – 1990S ARRIVAL [INTERVIEW 35]

53	R:	usted alguna vez le consiguió un trabajo a
54		alguien a través de contactos,
55	P:	Sí a ca:da rato
56	R:	A cada rato
57	P:	Sí
58	R:	qué gente recomienda,
59		(0.5)
60	P:	No: pues a la gente que:(h) verdaderamente necesite
61		el trabajo (y uno ve que) vea e(h) llame a esta
62		persona (.) .hh y:(h) y(h) él te va a decir que
63		trabajo es y:(h) bueno

The practice was reported by thirty-six out of thirty-eight participants. The frequency with which he describes the practice as illustrated by the adverbial expression *a ca:da rato*, ('all the time'/'constantly' l. 55), including the stretching and accentuation of the syllable 'a' in *cada*, inferentially conveys that solidarity is one of the social norms that underlie relations among co-ethnics (see Lucía's account in Example 1). As we will see later, this is one of the ways in which the actions of others are moralised as right or wrong. However, for solidarity to be extended to those seeking help, connections with the right contacts are needed, that is, those with some social capital within the social group. In addition, the help-seeker needs to meet certain requirements.

One of these requirements, as explained by Pablo and observed across many of my ongoing interactions with Latin Americans, including twenty-eight out of the thirty-eight interviews conducted, is often articulated as having a *la gente que verdaderamente necesite el trabajo* 'real need for work' (l. 60–1). At first sight, the implication (Grice, 1975) that not everyone who looks for employment really needs it is somewhat perplexing. If the person seeking employment did not need to work, they would not ask for help in the first place, let alone if they knew of any contacts that might be able to help. The presupposition that it entails is that being a co-ethnic or a co-national in need of work is not sufficient to be connected with others in the social group with whom the potential recommender is familiar.

Given that Latin Americans in London primarily work in the service sector in low-skilled jobs and often under exploitative conditions, what kind of attributes might be needed to effect such connections? In Example 4, Nélida, who first migrated from her native Cali to Spain, where she lived and worked as a nurse for ten years, offers us a glimpse of the kind of qualities that are required to obtain employment in the service sector. The interview was conducted in an eatery in one of the commercial clusters. Nélida was having lunch with Beatriz, a friend of hers who originally hailed from Bolivia and migrated to London via Buenos Aires, Argentina, where she lived for more than a decade.

Example 4. Nélida – post-2008 arrival [Interview 5][20]

228	B:	=Aparte ella es enfermera profesional
229	N:	Sí pero:(h) (.) aquí: (.) aquí soy ()(3.0)no
230		sé inglés (.) Hhehhhh
231	R:	Por eso (.) exactamente (.) sí ahí está el tema (.) y
232		cómo conseguiste el trabajo?
233		(2.0)
234	N:	Por mi amigo

[20] This interview was conducted in one of the eateries while the participants were having lunch. The long pauses observed coincided with the participants' consumption of food.

235	R:	Por tu amigo también
236	N:	el me trajo me recibió en su casa estuve
237		comiendo ahí donde él me dijo tranquila hasta que
238		consigas trabajo .hh () él mismo fue donde una
239		señora que era supervisora de una (madrugada) (0.8)
240		le dije yo lo que haya cualquier cosa (0.8)
241	R:	Claro=
242	N:	=entonces me llevó me presentó(y de una vez)al otro día
243		empecé a trabajar (.) con ella (.) ella misma como era
244		recomendada po:r mi amigo .hh que conocía a mi amigo
245		(2.3) ella misma me ofreció (.) otro trabajo los fines
246		de semana le dije listo yo los hago (.) ya prácticamente
247		yo hacía en semana (madrugada) (.) y sábado y domingo
248		trabajaba (1.2) y ya de ahí ya me fui organizando

Nélida would like to work as a nurse in London but rationalises her deskilling as a cleaner on the basis of her lack of English (*sí pero aquí soy (.) no sé inglés*, 'yes but here I (.) I don't speak English' l. 229–30). At the time when the interview was conducted, a Level 7 in International English Language Testing Service (IELTS) or a B grade in the Occupational English Test (OET) was required as well as registration with the Nursery and Midwifery council. This entailed a Test of Competence and an Objective Structured Clinical Examination. However, successful completion of these did not provide the right to work in the United Kingdom or guarantee a job at the end of it. The application process costs were circa £1,500[21] coupled with the costs Nélida would have to pay for English tuition. In line with many of the migrants I interacted with, Nélida is in stasis (Márquez Reiter, 2023). She is in a position that is unlikely to change. She has no access to affordable or accessible English provision given her antisocial work schedule and economic needs which make it very difficult to save such an amount of money.

Nélida thus had to resort to cleaning jobs as a way of sustaining herself in London. She explains that the willingness to accept cleaning jobs in the early hours of the morning and on weekends is what allowed her (l. 245–8) to lessen her dependency on her recommender. In other words, Nélida's agency, in line with that of the majority of the participants, is structured by her workplace function as she has become a means to productive outcomes (Urciuoli, 2016). As it emerged earlier in the interview, the recommender is a friend whom she helped while in Spain. Nélida's story echoes that of many

---

[21] www.nmc.org.uk/registration/joining-the-register/trained-outside-the-eueea.

Latin American migrants working under precarious conditions (thirty-six out of thirty-eight). For the purposes of this section, Nélida brings to the fore the flexibility that the job seeker is meant to show, and the importance of being recommended, in this case by the same person who made a recommendation for the cleaning supervisor who has now offered Nélida a job (1. 243–4). Although the supervisor did not know Nélida, a direct recommendation from the person who helped the supervisor obtain her job enhanced the chances of Nélida securing a cleaning position as Nélida is seen as potentially trustworthy (i.e., hard-working and discerning as to what information can and cannot be disclosed regarding the conditions of employment, see Section 4.3).

Nélida's donor (her recommender in London) is expected to help in accordance with the help he received from her while in Spain, that is, to vouch for her. The fulfilling of social obligations can help to balance out his credit. Earlier in the interview, Nélida explained that she provided a home for her now donor as he was a relative of a friend of hers in Cali and was homeless in Spain. In other words, the donor's recommendation represents a return of a favour. The original favour that Nélida did for her now donor, and that the donor did for the cleaning supervisor, has left a timeless imprint in the beneficiaries' minds (see, for example, Ledeneva, 2008). This means that it can be potentially reciprocated at any time to anyone that the original donor recommends. In this way the relationship between the original donor and the original beneficiary is further cemented.

However, the donor's social obligation is with their contact (the original provider of a favour of access) and not necessarily with the person their contact has recommended. In other words, the recommendation will not necessarily give the beneficiary, in this case Nélida, access to the supervisor's connections or guarantee Nélida's permanency in the job.

We have so far seen that: (1) solidarity is invoked as underlying the practice of recommendations and as a normative behavioural expectation among the participants in light of their common quest for mobility and the scarce resources at their disposal; (2) those with existing contacts in London prior to arrival have a better chance of securing help from co-ethnics; (3) the strength of the relationship with the contact is likely to determine the amount of help provided, especially when this involves a return of a favour; (4) the quality of contacts is important insofar as only those with some social capital in the group can effect help from others; and, (5) help-seekers need to meet certain requirements, such as having a real need for work and being good workers (e.g., perform their job at the highest standards, be flexible) and, as we will discuss next, possess the right work ethics (especially regarding keeping quiet about their conditions of employment in this largely unregulated sector of the economy).

4.3 Confidence in the Beneficiary's Work Ethics and Moral Character

Confidence in the beneficiary's work ethics and moral character was made evident during many of the interviews (twenty-nine out of thirty-eight). This is illustrated here in an interview with Liliana, a post-2000 migrant from Bogotá with limited knowledge of English, who received a telephone call from her work supervisor and left as soon as she drank her coffee.

EXAMPLE 5. LILIANA – POST-2000 ARRIVAL [INTERVIEW 38]

80	L:	Sí claro (.) en 40' más o menos llego
81	S:	[inaudible]
82	L:	Quédese tranquila que yo llego y lo hago
83	R:	Todo bien,
84	L:	Sí (.) qué pena pero me voy a tener que
85		ir (.) era mi supervisora justamente que
86		hay una vaina e-el trabajo y tengo que echarle una manita
87	R:	Los domingos trabajas,
88	L:	Normalmente no (.) pero parece que le faltó un cleaner
89	R:	Ajá
90	L:	Es que la supervisora me ha ayudado mucho a mí

Liliana represents what is understood within the social group as a 'good worker'. She is flexible, presumably hard-working, and prepared to be at the beck and call of her employer (i.e., the cleaning supervisor). Liliana justifies having to work on a Sunday afternoon out of the blue as a way to reciprocate the help she has received from her employer (*la supervisora me ha ayudado mucho a mí*, 'the supervisor has helped me a lot' l. 90). The favour of access provided by her supervisor does not have a time stamp. It is continually repaid by an adequate response. Doing so would help to repay the favour and add credit to Liliana's balance to help ensure that better work conditions and job opportunities may come her way. Liliana's views are further echoed by Julio, a post-2000 migrant from Armenia, Colombia.

Julio adds that being flexible and working well (l. 39–41), in this case thorough cleaning, not only helps to repay the favour but adds credit to his balance. It is likely to provide him with better working conditions, such as better shifts in terms of working hours, and potentially other jobs within the sector (l. 43, l. 45). As Julio explains, the benefits that attested good working ethics can provide him with are based on the favour received from his supervisor and on a rational calculation of the potential gains that might be accrued as a result of this, including maintaining the gravitas of the supervisor within the social group.

Example 6. Julio – post-2000 arrival [Interview 40]

32	R:	Qué tal tu trabajo,
33	J:	Pues bien (.) mi supervisor es buena gente y
34		colabora con uno así que cuando me pide algo estoy
35		a la orden
36	R:	En qué sentido,
37	J:	Pues lo que me pida le hago el favor
38	R:	Qué tipo de favores,
39	J:	una cava porque alguien no pudo ir a último
40		momento (.) o: que limpie lo que algún compañero
41		dejó mal pa que no haigan complaint después
42	R:	Ajá
43	J:	Y bue:no. así lo tienen en cuenta a uno
44	R:	Para qué,
45	J:	pa otros trabajos y pa la rota

Across the interviews conducted (thirty-eight out of thirty-eight), recommendations of second-order contacts are effected on the basis of the recommender's experience of having worked with the recommendee or having seen their performance at work. According to Ana, originally from Medellín and now retired, recommendations can only be performed when you trust the person that you are recommending.

Example 7. Ana – 1980s arrival [Interview 33]

32	R:	A quiénes recomiendas para trabajos
33	A:	Solo a la gente que conozco bien
34	R:	Qué es conocer bien,
35	A:	Pues a la gente de confianza
36	R:	Confianza,
37	A:	por ejemplo a familiares que sabes que trabajan
38		bien y no van a hacer las cosas mal <o a los que
39		no son familia pero sabes que trabajan bien>
40	R:	Y cómo sabes que trabajan bien=
41	A:	=porque los has visto trabajar (.) trabajaste con
42		ellos o una persona de tu confianza sabe que son

43		buenos
44	R:	Qué es trabajar bien para ti,
45	A:	no dar problemas (.) si te piden que hagas algo no
46		salir con la vaina ay yo no yo solo(.) trabajar a
47		conciencia

At lines 33, 35, and 37–9, Ana explicitly articulates the essential role that confidence in the recommendee's ability to work well plays in making recommendations possible and adds that trust is gained through lived work experience with the recommendee (l. 41–3). Thus, even first-order contacts may not meet the requirements needed for a recommendation to be instantiated, unless the recommender has attested their good worker's ethics. Good worker's ethics entails producing irreproachable results as measured in terms of productive outcomes (e.g., absence of complaints from the cleaning supervisor or the client) and the sharing of these behavioural codes. These involve being prepared to endure exploitation and engaging in hard labour: cleaning homes or offices with very short deadlines with few, if any, short breaks, and limited time to travel around the city to go from job to job. Ironically perhaps, transport journeys are used to find much-needed respite between jobs. Good worker's ethics allows for trust to be built. The development of trust, in turn, can enable further employment and business opportunities for those working as cleaners and those seeking to acquire more cleaning contracts, respectively. When the recommendee meets the work ethic expectations, the recommender obtains symbolic gains, such as an enhancement of their 'professional' reputation within the group (see also Example 10, l. 277–8). They are seen as someone who fully understands the labour market requirements in the sector of the economy where Latin Americans mainly work and is a good judge of character. It would then follow that recommending someone who does not meet the expectations of the service sector would damage the recommender's professional reputation and chances of obtaining potential material gains (see Example 10). Ana's views are echoed by Johan in Example 8.

On the topic of recommendations, Johan highlights the close relational connection that must exist between the recommender and the recommendee (l. 23, l. 25).

EXAMPLE 8. JOHAN – SECOND GENERATION [INTERVIEW 10]

22	R:	Recomendarías a alguien para algún trabajo
23	J:	tendría que tener una relación muy cercana o:(h)
24		conocer a esa persona haberla visto varias veces
25		trabajando a ver cómo es la persona(h) pero el resto
26		no .HH no no me atrevería a meter las manos al fuego
27		como decimos nosotros(.) pueda quedar uno mal.

In line with the previous accounts, he frames the relational connection with second-order contacts in terms of lived work experience and justifies it in terms of his own face concerns (Goffman, 1967). In keeping with the accounts provided by the participants of this study, for Johan, recommendations require having confidence in the recommendee's ability to work well. This, in turn, would allow the recommender to vouch for the recommendee. Johan articulates this via the expression *meter las manos en el fuego* (literally, 'stick your hands in fire', idiomatically, 'to stick one's neck out for somebody'. l. 26–7) and unpacks its potential consequences with explicit reference to face concerns: *pueda quedar mal uno* ('give one a bad image').

Indeed, face concerns were recurrently voiced when recounting practices of recommendations (in thirty-six out of thirty-eight interviews). They were articulated as one of the main risks involved in recommending someone to one's contacts.

EXAMPLE 9. CATALINA – 1990s MIGRANT [INTERVIEW 18]

45	R:	Has recomendado a alguien para algún trabajo,
46	C:	Uff un montón de veces
47	R:	Por ejemplo,
48	C:	A amigas de amigas, a gente con la que trabajé
49		antes pero hay que tener cuidado porque te pueden
50		hacer quedar mal
51	R:	En qué sentido
52	C:	Porque no hacen su trabajo bien y luego te hacen
53		quedar mal con la gente.
54	R:	Explícame un poquito eso
55	C:	Pues ya no puedes recomendar a nadie (.)te
56		pierden la confianza

In the words of Catalina, a 1990s migrant from Pereira in Example 9, the recommender can lose face if the recommendee is not up to the job (l. 49–50) as this may sully their good name or reputation. In this sense, therefore, the observed work ethics of prospective recommendees become a proxy for how they would perform on the job. In other words, confidence in the recommendee's work ethics becomes a risk-averse strategy, especially when favours of access need to be reciprocated. The recommendee's fulfilment of labour expectations becomes a testament of the recommender's capacity for judgement. When these are not met, the recommender risks losing the trust that they had gained (l. 56) with potential economic repercussions, such as being unable to place others in employment positions or securing further contracts, thus, potentially adversely affecting their livelihoods.

According to the participants, trust develops over accumulated relationships at work, especially in second-order relationships. As Catalina explains, recommending someone who lacks the expected work ethics in the sector can affect the trust that the recommender has achieved within the social group. This not only constitutes potential damage to their face but may also decrease the recommender's chances of further mobility (l. 55) inasmuch as it may sever the connections so far established. Dario, a 1990s migrant from Pereira, whom I had met twelve years ago, now has his own cleaning company. He explains that his mobility was achieved through the trust he had accumulated with co-ethnics and locals on the basis of his good work ethics and that of those whom he has recommended (l. 276–8).

EXAMPLE 10. DARIO – 1990S MIGRANT [INTERVIEW 15]

268	R:	Ajá muy bien .HH y: sé ahora que tienes un negocio
269		me dijo Norma .HH
270	D:	.hh sí ahora sí (ahora) tengo mi propia::(h) ()
271	R:	Tienes tu propi(o) emp[le-]
272	D:	[em]presa
273	R:	Tu propia empresa muy bien .HH y quién te ayudó a
274		montar la empresa?
275	D:	Hh M:::(h) a ver e:::(h) e::(h) com- e(h) esto(h)
276		esto(h) a ver te lo () y te lo () me vieron
277		trabajar no sé::(h) y la manera en que la gente que
278		yo ayudo a conseguir trabajos obra
279	R:	Sí .HH
280	D:	Y::(h) hh todo lo que me llegó (.) llegó de la nada
281		o sea::(h) fue:(h) .HH (.) trabajando bien
282		hablando con la misma gente con los mismos ingleses
283	R:	Sí=
284	D:	=e:::(h) creo que la confianza(h)
285	R:	Mj(h)
286	D:	que (vinieron en) hh en l(h) en la con la confianza
287		que .HH que cogieron (que vie-) que cogieron en mí
288	R:	Mj(h)
289	D:	Y me abrieron esa puerta y me dijeron (.) ellos a mí
290		.HH por qué usted no trabaja para nosotros? (.)
291		directamente .HH y por (es-) le digo abrí yo la
292		empresa
293	R:	M:(h)=
294	D:	=entonces las cosas se fueron dan- nunca(hh) e::(h)
295		(abrí) () .HH nunca:(h) toqué puertas (.) cada
296		persona me iba llamado(h) (.) ca- e:(h) pequeñas
297		me iban () en ese momento () (estás compuertas)
298		de oficinas
299	R:	Ajá

The virtuousness of being hard-working and committed to the job, despite often working under exploitative conditions, coupled with the irreproachable character of those whom he recommends have vested him with trust beyond co-ethnics. It has, in his own words, opened the doors to the external labour market (i.e., contracts outside the co-ethnic niche market) where he now has cleaning contracts that service non-Latin American businesses, such as offices and galleries. Dario articulates the mobility he has gained as a result of his hard work.

Dario explains that he did not have to do anything beyond what is required to achieve progress (1. 280–1). Progress achieved through quality connections is seen as a consequence of virtuous labour rather than simply solidarity. In describing his achieved occupational mobility in causal terms, Dario paints a picture of himself as a non-agentive relative to those who helped him. Dario explains that he did not have to knock on any doors to progress. He did not have to do anything besides doing a good job. Thus, once again, we observe how agency is structured by the workplace. Despite the constraining and limiting dimensions of the workplace, these are accepted, and economic mobility is envisaged as possible based on being seen as dedicated and hard-working. This is evidenced in the way in which he articulates his achieved mobility with the impersonal construction *me abrieron esa puerta*, 'that door was opened for me' (1. 289), where the subject is not determined given that it is this very subject, in this case the locals (i.e., 'the English'), who have the ability to execute such actions. The expression denotes that the door that was opened was not any door but the gateway to possibilities, as illustrated by the choice of the distal deictic *esa* ('that'). In the case of Dario, this gateway represents access to the external labour market. This allows him to mediate access to the internal labour market of those whom he employs, principally co-ethnics. Dario has thus become a gatekeeper: he connects co-ethnics with others needing to fill positions in the service sector. Dario adds that access to the gateway of mobility 'reached him' with the object pronoun construction *me llegó*, which he later increments with 'came out of nowhere' (*llegó de la nada*, 1. 280). In so doing, he depicts himself as the rightful recipient of the benefits that confidence in one's ability to work conscientiously and be dedicated to the job brings. Hard work is thus portrayed again as a precursor to gaining trust and the latter as a catalyst for progress.

The analysis so far has shown that solidarity is seen as one of the values that permeates, or ought to permeate (see Patricia in Example 2), relations among co-ethnics. It is invoked in the provision of favours of access, especially in instantiating recommendations. Despite the moral value assigned to solidarity, in practice, solidarity among co-ethnics who have undergone similar or worse circumstances in diaspora, or indeed those who have a first-order relationship with a potential recommender, is not necessarily sufficient to leverage connections. The notion of solidarity has acquired a different meaning for the Latin Americans in this study. In the circumstances of general immobility and precariousness (Butler, 2012) in which the participants of this study tend to live, it goes hand in hand with the development of trust. Kinship or a shared migration trajectory does not suffice to avail oneself of favours of access (cf. Mouw, 2003). While having quality contacts within the social group enhances the chances of obtaining job information and can influence the help received from one's social ties (Granovetter, 1995), trust in the recommendee's ability to work well is needed to obtain (better) job opportunities. Trust is achieved by attested work ethics and is seen as essential for occupational recommendations and positive change. If the recommendee falls short of the labour expectations, the recommender may lose face within the group and, as result, hamper their chances of obtaining future material gains.

The analysis has also revealed that as a way of expressing their gratitude for obtaining better working conditions, such as cleaning jobs that pay over the minimum wage, migrant workers report working extra hard to honour the recommendation and the possibility of professional growth. In other words, they strive to maintain the work ethics for which they hope to be known as a means of gaining further opportunities. Hard work and job dedication constitute some of the values that connect Latin American migrants with one another, in particular those in second-order relationships, especially but not limited to the Colombian participants of this study. The workplace is one of the sites where relationships are forged. Importantly, having such attributes can aid the maintenance of relationships and economic mobility. It is thus not surprising to hear the discourse of Colombians as good workers that circulates among Latin Americans, expectedly among Colombians themselves.

4.4 Colombians Work Well

The discourse of Colombians as good workers recurrently surfaces across the interviews (in thirty-five out of thirty-eight interviews). Susana, in Example 11, had been in London for six years when interviewed and had studied industrial design in her home country. Susana had worked as a cleaner on arrival, then as a waitstaff and later as a volunteer in a Colombian overseas mission, where she had heard of her current part-time position. She hoped that her volunteering would open the doors to opportunities outside the service industry.

EXAMPLE 11. SUSANA – POST-2000 MIGRANT [INTERVIEW 1]

```
65   R:   Y en tu experiencia cómo se consigue trabajo
66        en Londres,
67   S:   E:(h) yo creo que eh (.) todo el mundo viene
68        con la misma mentalidad (.) todo el mundo tiene
69        situaciones personales diferentes entonces por
70        ejemplo unas personas (0.4) que tiene apoyo
71        económico por ejemplo desde Colombia es mucho más
72        fácil () (.) los otros de voz a voz
74   R:   =ajá=
75   S:   =(yo creo) que se enamoran pues (del trabajo) (
76        porque) los colombianos son muy buenos
78        Trabajar es un problema () como organizaciones(.) .HH
79        que o empiezas limpia:ndo empiezas siendo mesero y tienes
80        que pagar ()y tienes que hacer
81        y- y- no puedes dejar ese trabajo porque y- y- ya
82        (0.1) te quedas ahí es muy difícil salir de ahí
83        (LO ES) (0.1).hh entonces yo me daba cuenta de
84   R:   °Sí°
85   S:   Pero nosotros ya (conoces) el medio (.) y::(h)
86        podrías ayudar a la gente pues () aunque ()
87        que es: (.) la visa (.) y el permiso de trabajo
88   R:   Y cómo consiguen trabajo
89   S:   °de voz a voz°
```

Susana explains that those without quality transnational connections – that is, those without a contact in Colombia who can either put the help-seeker in touch with connections in London to provide help prior to migrating, on and/or after arrival, or receive financial assistance from Colombia (l. 70–2) – are at a disadvantage and obtain work through word of mouth (l. 72). Susana also describes the general immobility and stasis that, unlike her, these migrants face through othering, as illustrated in the use of the third-person plural *son* 'they are' rather than the first-person plural *somos* 'we are' at l. 76. Susana explains that while these migrant workers might be able to progress, at least socially, from cleaning to serving in restaurants, they are unlikely to break the chains of servitude they are under given their economic needs and lack of quality connections (l. 79–82).

Susana adds that the work carried out by Colombians in relation to cleaning is such that the employers fall in love with their work (l. 75). Through this exaggeration (Drew, 2003), Susana strengthens the high quality of Colombian labour in the service sector relative to that of other unspecified cultural groups. Her exaggeration, however, should be understood in the context of Latin American migration to London. As explained in

Section 3, Colombians were the majority of early Latin American arrivals and constitute the largest group of Spanish-speaking Latin Americans in London. This enabled them to avail themselves of opportunities that later arrivals did not necessarily have, such as free ESOL provision and more lax immigration laws, which allowed some of them to obtain regular status, and in many cases, British citizenship. Regular status enabled many Colombians to clean offices rather than just private homes. Nevertheless, knowledge gained from ongoing ethnographic work and interactions with Latin Americans in London indicates that those in an irregular position can also avail themselves of the required documentation (e.g., a national insurance number), to clean government or private offices (see Márquez Reiter and Kádár, 2022 for an interview where this practice is disclosed), albeit at a financial cost and personal risk.

Irrespective of the situation of irregularity that many Colombians, as well as other (non) Latin American migrants, find themselves in, they nevertheless obtain cleaning jobs in offices via relevant recommendations. In these cases, the co-ethnic cleaning supervisor or a friend whom they trust provides them with the right documentation to work in the United Kingdom. Typically, the documentation belongs to another migrant – preferably of the same gender and approximate age as the worker and ideally of Spanish-speaking origin[22] – who hire out their regular documents to be used for a set of working hours that will not exceed those that the 'lender' is allowed to perform for tax purposes. The worker may not necessarily know the owner of the documentation, and typically pays his employer a percentage of their earnings for this 'favour' of access. It is thus not uncommon to use different documents in different jobs, that is, to clean an office building using one identity and another under a different one. The practice of kickbacks through which employment is illicitly facilitated in exchange for payment requires a high level of trust. Not least because the worker has entered an (im)moral oath and will thus have to conform to it, even in those cases where the agreed payment differs from the wage received. In the words of a long-standing friend and helper of Latin Americans in London, originally from Belize, 'Colombians hire each other because they know they will keep schtum'; that is, they will not disclose the practices through which they were hired.

Despite typically paying over the minimum wage, private home cleaning is generally more labour-intensive and rarely subject to contract.[23] Office

---

[22] This preference responds to the potentiality of Home Office checks where the workers may need to justify their identity.

[23] Private home cleaning is generally seen as hard work relative to office cleaning despite the early hours of the morning in which the latter is usually carried out. Private home cleaning tends to be articulated as spit and polish compared to the general dusting and vacuuming of office cleaning.

cleaning, on the other hand, is seen as a potential avenue for some progress, albeit rather limited given some of the exigencies of the job, such as working in the early hours of the morning and often having to clean offices located in different points of the city. Through conscientious work (see Example 7), migrants may progress to cleaning supervisory positions, including running their own cleaning companies (see Example 10) where they tend to employ co-ethnics (see Example 4) and, as we will see later, principally co-nationals.

According to an onward migrant from Spain who had been in London for ten years when interviewed and is originally from Santa Cruz, Bolivia, 'Colombians >who are the majority< reign in this country (.) the [cleaning] supervisors are all Colombian (.) they are in control and give each other the jobs'. While many cleaning supervisors are of Colombian origin, the participants of this study also report working for supervisors who are Brazilian, Ecuadorian, and, in a few cases, of African descent. Besides the intercultural tensions to which this onward migrant alludes (Patiño-Santos and Márquez Reiter, 2019), my interactions with Latin Americans in London over the years, coupled with the accounts gathered across the life-story interviews conducted for this study, confirm that Colombians tend to employ co-nationals whom they trust, either because they have witnessed that they are 'good workers' or through word of mouth from someone they trust. In this sense, therefore, Susana's exaggeration at line 75 highlights the importance that a job well done can have for further employment opportunities. It does, however, bring into question the alleged lovability of the work performed by Colombians. It shines some light on intercultural relations among Latin Americans in London and points to a potential further requirement for work recommendations to be instantiated: being a co-national.

Subsequently in the interview, as illustrated in Example 12, Susana notes how connecting job seekers with potential employers in London works by contrasting it with the way it works in Colombia.

EXAMPLE 12. SUSANA – POST-2000 MIGRANT [INTERVIEW 1] CONTINUED

90	S:	en Colombia pues (sólo como que eres mi)
91		amigo vas a conseguir trabajo (0.1).HH pero aquí:(h)
92		yo recomiendo mis amigos () (lo recomiendo como
93		persona lo conozco)(.) pero el proceso e:s totalmente
94		decisión de ellos y: he recomendado algunos >()
95		(trabajan y otros no)<=
96	R:	=y por qué te parece que pasa eso

Various participants described their cleaning jobs in offices as *trabajar pa' que digan por aquí pasó* ('work so that they notice that the cleaner has been') and *limpiar lo que ve la suegra* (literally: 'clean what the mother-in-law sees', idiomatically: 'clean superficially').

97	S:	.HH creo que la gente es más- más (.) regular en
98		ese tipo de cosas (y los procesos y la gente lo
99		siente.) (.) creo que el inglés () no porque
100		Sea tu amiga quiere decir que trabaje bien (.)()
101		me caes muy bien pero=
102	R:	=y entre Colombianos?
103	S:	() (.) porque es diferente si tu vas a
104		u::n: trabajo de limpieza por ejemplo (.) tú no
105		necesitas referencia de ningún tipo (.) .hh al
106		menos que te conozcan (.) que te pregunten sabes
107		limpiar? yo no sabía pero yo dije que sí porque
108		tú puedes mopear el piso o lavar un baño(.) .hh
109		okey yo la conozco e:(h)mh es confiable (para que) la
110		tomes() entonces es: (0.2) es depende dónde
111		estés

She explains that in Colombia the relational tie between the recommender with the job seeker (i.e., a relationship of friendship) and with the potential employer is what determines job seekers' success in obtaining employment. She thus suggests that other factors, such as the ability to carry out the job effectively, may occupy a secondary position. In so doing, Susana alludes to the practice of *palanca* vis-à-vis the way in which job recommendations work in London. Friends are also recommended in London, but the chances of securing a position are not simply subject to the relational connection between the recommender and the recommendee or between the former and the potential employer. Although the recommendee has received help from a contact of their contact (i.e., the employer) to access a job, the help is temporal. In other words, the recommendee will have to comply with the work expectations to maintain the job and establish a relationship with the recommender to avail themselves of further work opportunities via recommendations.

When I asked Susana for her views on why she would only recommend people whom she knows and why she was confident they would perform well (l. 97), she responded by contrasting the fairness and procedural regularity that guides the behaviour of the locals, referred to as 'the English'. This 'fairness' and 'procedural regularity' are, however, otiose for office cleaning contracts are generally outsourced; hence, the responsibility to employ the 'right' people for the job lies with the contractor. The locals (i.e., 'the English'), in contrast to Colombians back home, objectively assess the job seeker's qualities relative to Latin Americans. Besides her stance on recruitment procedures in Colombia versus the United Kingdom, she explains that the kind of blue-collar jobs that Colombians perform in London do not require any kind of references as they entail unskilled labour

(l. 106–9). She does, however, stress that a recommendation is nonetheless required: knowing that the job seeker is trustworthy (*yo la conozco e:(h)mh es confiable (para que) la tomes*, 'I know her u:(h)mh she is trustworthy (so that) you can hire her', l. 110–11).

Trust in the ability of the recommendee to conform to the expected work ethics figures once again as a condition for effecting recommendations. Susana's mention of trustworthiness, however, is not directly connected with the hard-working abilities of the recommender or the quality of labour given that anyone can do such jobs (l. 109 cf. Example 11, l. 75). As the interaction with Susana was coming to a close, she asked me for more details about the research project (l. 181, l. 184-Example 13). Upon hearing about my interest in relationships among Latin Americans (l. 182–3) and, more specifically, *palanca* (l. 185–6), Susana repeats the term, albeit softly, followed by loud laughter (l. 187). With this she signals her metapragmatic interpretation of our preceding talk and proceeds to offer information on the relationships between Colombians in London.

EXAMPLE 13. SUSANA – POST-2000 MIGRANT [INTERVIEW 1] CONTINUED

181	S:	Y acerca de qué es exactamente tu proyecto
182	R:	Es para un libro sobre las relaciones entre los
183		latinoamericanos en Londres
184	S:	Qué?
185	R:	Específicamente estoy interesada en el tema de la
186		palanca
187	S:	°la palanca(h)° (.) HHEHHEHHEHH
188	R:	Sí.
190	S:	Primero (.) puede ser que (alguien) llegues a algún
191		lugar y:(h)(.) por ser colombiano
192		un colombiano contrate a otro que sea colombiano
193	R:	Colombiano contrate colombiano=
194	S:	=yo diría que sí
195	R:	Y por qué te parece
196	S:	yo creo que porque conoce (su gente) ()
197		procesos de aprendizaje de las personas saben cómo
198		trabajan .HH y creo que es muy difícil
199		para algunas personas: (.) la interrelación
200		con las otras culturas?
201	R:	Mj(h)
202	S:	Entonces tratar con un (polaco) es diferente tratar
203	S:	con un español es diferente
204		todo el mundo tiene procesos de aprendizaje
205		y de trabajo diferentes .HH y a veces la gente
206		() lo mismo(h) .HH pero igual depende de tu
207		medio y de tu mercado

Susana rationalises the likelihood of obtaining employment from a Colombian co-national on the basis of similar cultural expectations rather than the 'attractiveness' of Colombian labour (see Example 11, l. 75). From an understanding of culture couched in national terms, Susana explains that cultural expectations may not be shared across cultures. According to Susana, therefore, the hiring of Colombians by Colombians is presented as responding to the intercultural problems that may arise from working with those from different cultural backgrounds. Although she entertains the possibility of difference between Colombians (l. 205–6), the practice of hiring co-nationals is presented as a risk-averse strategy to ensure expected work ethics. Thus, despite its rationalisation, the expected rules of behaviour at work once again figure as an important factor for obtaining work. Susana explains that trust in the recommendee's work ethics is essential for recommendations to work, as shown in Example 14.

EXAMPLE 14. SUSANA – POST-2000 MIGRANT [INTERVIEW 1] CONTINUED

208	R:	Te parece que la palanca funciona aquí
209	S:	Yo creo que la recomendación funciona(h)
210		pero:(h)(0.1) en estos trabajos(0.2) como te digo
211		yo (.) he(h) intentado ayudar a mucha gente mucha
212		gente (he tenido que) () otros () dicen que
213		me quieren mucho que °() no funciona
214		y()funciona° (0.1)y está bien y es respetable y el-
215		respeto mucho los procesos y prefiero que sea así
216		para(h) (0.4) te la traigo la conoces ()
217		pero es tu decisión si la contratas () hhhh=
218	R:	=claro
219	S:	>Tú cabeza(hh) hhehh<
220		=Sí es porque bueno (pensás que) Y:(h) (.) hay un
221		Un riesgo ahí y es (.) que tú pierdes la capacidad
222		de recomendar a otra persona

From line 216, Susana narrates the way in which recommendations work, whereby the potential employer is under no social or moral obligation to hire the recommendee. Put differently, the 'lending of the contact' to the recommendee is not alienable. It is thus up to the recommendee to demonstrate their moral worth in terms of work ethics to secure the position. Susana also notes that when this does not happen, the recommender loses face insofar as their capacity to make other recommendations is curtailed. Trust is thus an essential condition for recommendations to be effected. The recommendee needs to be trusted in terms of their work ethics to gain a favour of access by the recommender, and the latter's judgement is endorsed by the attested work ethics of the former. One of the ways in which the risk of potential face loss is managed is by hiring co-nationals who share similar norms and work expectations.

As mentioned earlier, the favour of access that the recommendee received from the recommender is not transferable. There is no social obligation from the employer to the recommendee. The latter will have to work hard to establish their connection with the employer by performing their job according to the expected work ethics, that is, the rules of work conduct. This, in turn, will help them accrue the moral worth needed to progress, such as better work opportunities or further recommendations (see Example 6). In those cases where the recommendee does not meet the expected work ethics, the recommender may lose face (see Example 8 and Example 9, and also Example 12), with implications for their relationship with the contact, in this case the employer, and their professional reputation in the community.

Susana's views coincide with those of many of the Colombians who arrived in the 1980s and 1990s and have had their own businesses in London. Juan Carlos, in Example 15, arrived in the 1980s following the political turmoil in his native Manizales. He initially worked delivering homemade *quesito paisa* (soft cheese) for a Paisa co-national and later added *arepas* (corn cakes) and *pandebono*[24] to his delivery menu to cater for the palate of later Colombian arrivals. Juan Carlos learnt of an opening in one of the commercial clusters through his Paisa employer and decided to open an eatery with his then wife. Juan Carlos was interviewed during the slow hours of the eatery while drinking a cup of coffee. The staff at his eatery spoke Spanish featuring various Colombian accents. During our interaction, an onward migrant from Spain, as evidenced by her communicative repertoire,[25] approached us asking for work. On witnessing this, I asked Juan Carlos if he hires people to work for him (l. 88).

---

[24] *Quesito paisa* is fresh soft cheese usually found in *arepas* and typical of the Antioquia region. *Pandebono* is made of corn flour, cassava starch, cheese, and eggs and is typical of the Valle del Cauca region. His addition of *pandebono* to the menu offers an indirect portrait of early Colombian migration to London.

[25] This was observed, among others, by the level of directness, including the use of the informal second-person singular, with which she approached Juan Carlos to ask for any available positions *Perdona tienes algún puesto aquí* ('Excuse me do you have any posts here').

EXAMPLE 15. JUAN CARLOS – LATE 1980S ARRIVAL [INTERVIEW 13]

88 R: tú: contratas gente aquí a trabajar?=
89 C: =(hay veces)=
90 R: =recomendados=
91 C: =°(casi siempre)°=
92 R: =y qué tipo de gente?=
93 C: =latinos
94 R: Por qué latinos?
95 C: Porque es un sitio latino
96 R: alguna preferencia?
97 C: Los colombianos () (.) colom-=
98 R: =y por qué colombianos?
99 C: Los conozco (.) me relaciono bien con ellos y son dinámicos entiendes?
       Y vienen recomendados

In line with the views of Susana and those expressed by other Colombian interviewees, knowledge of the culture in national terms (Roth, 2016) is an important factor in obtaining employment, as are recommendations. The expectation of those who hail from the same country and have similar migration trajectories (see Example 2) is that they understand each other and the exigencies of the segmented labour market in which they are inserted. They will thus be expected to be 'dynamic' (l. 99) despite having to hold various jobs, often in different locations, on the same day. They are also willing to be at the beck and call of their employers to earn the necessary moral worth to make a living in London relative to other migrant groups with whom complex social relations are indicated (see Example 2, Example 14, and Example 15). Colombians are generally depicted by the Colombian participants of this study as trustworthy, hence, as potentially recommendable. Ethnographic work conducted over the years with Latin Americans in London offers a complementary side to these accounts, especially as far as how trust is constructed.

4.5 Concluding Remarks

In the analysis presented, the process of how the situated practice of work recommendations is effected has been elucidated through the participants' reflections. Recommendations consitute a speech event, and we have seen a set of conditions need to be met for its successful performance. Thus, it is essential that the recommendee is in need of employment and that they consider that the recommender can broker employment for them based on their relevant diasporic connections. Similarly, the recommender predicts that the recommendee will accept the offer of employment and believes that they are prepared to work under the precarious conditions that characterise this sector of the economy. We have also seen that the recommendee must possess the expected work ethics (as attested by the donor or by word of mouth from someone trustworthy and will keep quiet about any employment-related irregularities). Finally, the recommender believes that the recommendation will be beneficial. That is, when these conditions are met, the recommendee will secure employment and be in debt with the recommender for the favour of access received. The recommendee will be obliged to meet the work expectations of the employer to continue being employed and accrue the trust needed to be recommended for other work opportunities – either by the original recommender, the current employer, or work colleagues who can attest to their work ethics. When these are met, the recommender increases their gravitas, especially among their social contacts, and the primary economic order on which the social group is constituted is maintained. We have also seen that while being a first-order contact or a co-national may increase the chances of a work recommendation, these factors alone do not guarantee that a favour of access will be effected. In simple terms, first-order contacts and co-nationals need to meet the very same conditions, contrary to how the practice of *palanca* has been reported to work back home.

These conditions are based on the understanding that behavioural codes, as far as normative work expectations are concerned, are shared between the donor and the beneficiary, that they will allow the latter to perform their duties and the donor to maintain their professional face within the social group. In simple terms, they are based on the confidence that the donor has on the beneficiary's ability and preparedness to perform according to the requirements of the niche economy where most Latin Americans are inserted. In other words, they are based on trust. Therefore, trust is not a given even in those cases where the beneficiary may be a first-order contact of the donor (see Section 4.3). Trust is constructed on the basis of observed work performance and allows for the potential development of further employment opportunities.

As explained earlier, an occupational recommendation represents a favour of access provided by the donor in connecting the beneficiary with one of their contacts. For the favour of access to be granted, the donor needs to have confidence in the beneficiary's ability and preparedness to comply with the economic sector's requirements. The relational connection provided is, however, inalienable. This means that the beneficiary will need to abide by the expected work ethics in order to build their own moral personhood, that is to accrue their own moral worth. This, in turn, can lead to more or better employment opportunities within the sector, help to sustain the beneficiary's relationship with the donor and the donor's relationship with their contact, and perpetuate the labour chain.

The favour of access bestowed leaves a timeless stamp that needs to be continually repaid. It is not paid in gratitude but paid 'in kind' somewhere else in their working sphere. This is done by fulfilling socially normative behaviour in the working sphere, that is, having the 'right' work ethics. Work ethics, in this context, conflate expected behavioural norms with social oughts (cf. Culpeper and Tantucci, 2021 on reciprocity as a proto moral social credit-debit principle of (im)politeness). They enable the beneficiary to secure and keep their employment, the donor and the beneficiary to maintain their professional face within the social group and, provide fertile ground for further economic opportunities that go beyond the benefits that the donor and the beneficiary received through the enactment of favour access.

In this setting, optimally appropriate relationships are those which make sure that the economic order on which the livelihood of the social group is constituted is not upset. In other words, the moral worth of members of the social group is evaluated according to what they are prepared to do and not necessarily on who they know. In view of this, the moral order on which relations are built and leveraged for occupational mobility is based on 'a generally shared understanding of where one's and other's actions sit within the spectrum of "right" and "wrong" behaviours' (Márquez Reiter, 2022) to secure a livelihood and ensure that the livelihoods of others within the group are not negatively impacted. This means that attending to one's needs simultaneously involves attending to those of the collective (cf. Márquez Reiter, 2021). This is because the organisation of the social group is contingent on highly unequal socio-economic realities. It then follows that the main condition for the performance of occupational recommendations presupposes the need of the sector of the labour market where members of the social group are mainly inserted.

5 Conclusion

The case study presented in this Element has made an original contribution to the social side of pragmatics by being the first to give voice to the lived experiences of relationality of economic migrants as they try to sustain their livelihoods away from home. In particular, it has contributed to understanding how Spanish-speaking Latin Americans in London, a largely under-represented social group whose presence is highly visible in parts of the capital, leverage and maintain social ties within their social group to advance their well-being under harsh social and economic circumstances.

Reflexive accounts gathered through interviews with members of this social group and insights from ethnographic fieldwork revealed the pivotal role of relational connections as a way of securing employment and making a living. They shone a light on some of the connections between the practice of *palanca* back home and the diasporic relational practice of co-ethnic occupational recommendations. First-order contacts, regardless of their time of arrival, are more likely to be recommended for jobs. However, unlike *palanca*, first-order contacts will have to show their economic worth and demonstrate that they are trustworthy.

Being a relative or a close friend of the recommender, rather than an acquaintance, can facilitate occupational recommendations, at least initially, given that such interpersonal bonds often entail the expectation of solidarity and involve a certain degree of trust. However, the conditions of the sector of the economy where members of this social group are incorporated require the establishment and continual construction of trust between the recommender and the recommendee as well as between the latter, their employer, and those whom they work with. Confidence in the recommendee's work ethics and general moral character is earned based on their attested work performance, either by the recommender or by word of mouth by trusted members of the social group who have witnessed the recommendee's commitment to work. Trust in the recommendees and indeed in their agency are contingent on their ability to generate productive outcomes for the recommender, themselves, and others in their social group. Indeed, failure to reciprocate the favour of access may be sanctioned by exclusion from the co-ethnic niche economy. The beneficiary's behaviour is thus oriented to their obligation and interdependence with the social group (see Portes 1998). Behaviour in line with the normative expectations of a social group primarily inserted in the largely informal service economy helps to sustain the group's economic viability.

While solidarity is invoked as underlying the practice of work recommendations and as a normative behavioural expectation, we have seen how migrants (first-, second-generation, or onward migrants) with pre-existing social contacts in London prior to arrival, especially contacts with social capital, have a better chance of securing help from co-ethnics. We have, nonetheless, noted that first- and second-generation Latin Americans find work recommendations less challenging than onward migrants without pre-existing social contacts in London. This responds to the diasporic connections they have made based on their length of settlement in London, the tacit knowledge they have of the social group's expectations, and conditions of the co-ethnic niche economy.

The amount of help beneficiaries receive depends on the strength of the relationship, especially when a return of a favour is involved. Notwithstanding this, recommendees must meet certain structural requirements such as having a 'real need' for work and possessing the right work ethics to receive help. We have attested how solidarity goes hand in hand with the development of trust. In other words, kinship or a shared migration trajectory does not suffice to avail oneself of favours of access (cf. Mouw, 2003). Instead, trust is achieved by attested work ethics (i.e., the rules of conduct within the social group). Falling short of the expected work ethics may sully the recommender's name and hamper the chances of obtaining future material gains. To put it in another way, recommendees (first-, second-generation, and onward migrants) who do not behave in line with the behaviour expected of them are punished (i.e., they are fired or unlikely to be recommended for other work opportunities), and their actions can negatively affect the good name of the recommender and the livelihood of others within the group. On the contrary, the recommendee's adherence to the actions expected of them enhances the recommender's professional reputation in the social group as someone whose dicta can be trusted.

In addition, we have observed how an original favour of access marks a potential new stage in the interpersonal relationship between the recommender and the recommendee. Furthermore, we have noted how the original favour of access leaves a timeless imprint on the recommendee's mind. The recommendee will thus be in debt with the recommender, hence likely to oblige to their (work) demands. We have also seen that contacts provided by the recommender are not transferable; that is to say, recommendations will not give the recommendee access to the circle (vs. *palanca*).

Relationships within the social group are embedded in a primarily transactional order in the light of the social and economic conditions under which members of the social group have to make a living. In this context, then, optimally appropriate relations are principally defined by the economic value individuals bring to the social group. It then follows that the role of individuals in their relationships with others within the group is evaluated in terms of their capacity to produce productive economic outcomes for all. Adherence to the expected work ethics and to the requirements of a largely unregulated sector of the economy characterised by exploitation and precarity means that the moral order on which the group is based is not upset.

Overall, the study has demonstrated the importance of relationality in a contemporary context of globalisation for livelihood sustenance. This is a social reality which affects millions of people all over the world but one which pragmaticists have not provided sufficient attention until now, despite it being one of the biggest societal challenges facing the globe. I have shown that the interconnectedness between migrants, and potentially between non-migrants too, goes beyond the dyadic relationships that pragmatics has traditionally concentrated on. I have maintained that the interpersonal relationships and the rights and obligations of their incumbents should be examined by considering the wider relational context in which they are embedded as well as the place which they occupy within wider societal structures. Ignoring such contextual information and the main purpose of the interactions between the language users we examine can distort the analyses we offer.

The Element has connected pragmatics with knowledge from the social sciences, with special attention to issues of (im)mobility in a diasporic context entrenched in inequalities, especially as far as accessing resources is concerned. This coupled with ethnographic knowledge gained via observations through ongoing work with Latin Americans in London, the gathering of documentary evidence, and the conducting of interviews have enabled us to understand how the participants of this study make sense of their relations with others within the group, know their importance in their everyday lives, and comprehend the practices they reported as situated in the light of the structural dimensions they experience.

The case study offered here has evidenced that work recommendations are activities of everyday life where the moral order is reconstituted under insurmountable structural conditions. The norms on which this moral order is based are used to evaluate the moral personhood of others, as we have seen, for example, by the work ethics expected of co-ethnics. Recommendations represent an active fulfilment of the moral obligations that Colombians, as well as other Latin Americans, in London have towards each other. Drawing on Lambek (2015: 18), recommendations constitute 'actions embedded in a cycle of the production and cancellation of particular, personal, interpersonal and collective states'. They re-establish 'the criteria through which persons and relationships are constituted and the world renewed'.

In this Element I have thus sought to expand the horizon of pragmatic research by offering a first sociopragmatic inquiry into the sociocultural norms that underlie the establishment and maintenance of interpersonal relations of a given social group in a context of social injustice. Beyond the specificity of the examples drawn from the experience of Latin American migrants in London, the findings are likely to resonate with other economic migrants inhabiting similar structural conditions or indeed with other segregated and under-represented social groups. In this sense, therefore, the Element raises opportunities for further research, in terms of comparisons both with members of other marginalised social groups but also within the same social group. For instance, further research on the role of transdiasporic relations (i.e., between migrants across diasporic locales) would help to refine and further elaborate on the novel findings presented here. Similarly, the study could be extended by interrogating the role of new information and technology in facilitating the migration journey but also in maintaining ties with their home countries and helping integration into the receiving societies.

Finally, it is my sincere hope that this Element will foster a dialogue among like-minded scholars to move pragmatics beyond its primarily middle-class milieu and address more explicitly current societal challenges. The theme addressed in this Element – how diasporic relationships are leveraged for livelihood sustenance – and the issues addressed never cease. They are in constant flux. Reattending to them will allow us to further elaborate on them and attest their relevance to the other communicative contexts.

Appendix
Transcription Conventions

[	beginning of overlap
]	end of overlap
	underlining of (part of) words indicates some form of stress or emphasis
=	latching
-	indicates a cut off of the prior word or sound
::	indicates pitch rise'volume' is indicated with capital letters
()	indicates that the talk or item could not be heard
(0.3)	numbers in parentheses indicate silence represented in tenths of a second

EXAMPLES – translations into English

TRANSLATION OF EXAMPLE 1. LUCIA – ONWARD MIGRANT [INTERVIEW 7]

58 R: *and your friends where did you know them from Medellin*
59 L: *From:: (h) Colombia yes*
60 R: *From Colombia itself (.) and::m:: and are you still in*
61   *contact with them?*
62 L: *Yes*
63 R: *=they live here to=*
64 L: *=aha=*
65 R: *=ok (.) and: have you needed help to see a doctor*
66   *a denti:st=*
67 L: *=u:::(h) (there) always of course (.) consider that we*
68   *don't speak English*
69 R: *And who helped you*
70 L: *Well everyone (0.3) when one arrives here:(h)m*
71   *(.) .hh see who can accompany me here ()*
72   *someone recommends a person and that person another(and one)*
73   *I've been accompanied .HH (.) by so many people that I cannot*
74   *remember how many (.) for all the things*
75   *one has to do when you arrive*

TRANSLATION OF EXAMPLE 2. PATRICIA – ONWARD MIGRANT [INTERVIEW 24]

80	P:	*So they discriminate people who arrive now and*
81		*as we arrive last then they have a little*
82		*advantage already and they want::(h) I mean to take*
83		*from us because we: if one is going to ask for a favour*
84		*yes I do it for you but I charge so much. HH for a*
85		*simple call (.)it's (even) inhu- inhumane that*
86		*they charge for a call among comrades we are away from*
87		*our countries and .HH [but well this is life]*
88	R:	*[but are they Colombians] that*
89		*have been here all their lives=*
90	P:	*=that have been here all their lives yes they have been*
91		*here for forty thirty five years*
92	R:	*Yes yes I know*
93	P:	*But unfortunately it's like this that (object pronoun repeated)*
94		*bothers me a lot because look I say now*
95		*if we are all in the same struggle we all want to*
96		*get out from .hh why do we do that? Why can't we*
97		*give a little hand if it doesn't cost anything to make*
98		*a call from my own phone (.) but they charge you then*
99		*right: that upsets me a lot you know?. HH*

TRANSLATION OF EXAMPLE 3. PABLO – 90S-ARRIVAL [INTERVIEW 35]

53	R:	*have you ever found a job for*
54		*someone through your contacts,*
55	P:	*Yes a:ll the time*
56	R:	*All the time*
57	P:	*Yes*
58	R:	*Who do you recommend,*
59		*(0.5)*
60	P:	*No: well people who: (.)really need*
61		*the job (and that one sees) look u(m) call this*
62		*person (.) .hh and: (h) he is going to tell you*
63		*what the job is and: (h) that's it*

TRANSLATION OF EXAMPLE 4. NÉLIDA – POST-2008 ARRIVAL [INTERVIEW 5]

228	B:	=*besides she is a professional nurse*
229	N:	*Yes but: (h) (.) here: (.) here I am ()(3.0) I don't*
230		*know English (.)Hhehhh*
231	R:	*that's why (.) exactly (.) that is the issue (.) and*
232		*How did you find the job?*
233		*(2.0)*
234	N:	*through a friend*
235	R:	*through your friend too*
236	N:	*the one that brought me and lodged me*
237		*and fed me and he told me don't worry until you*
238		*find work .hh ()he himself went to see a*
239		*a woman that was a supervisor in the (early mornings)(0.8)*
240		*I said to him that I'd take anything available (0.8)*
241	R:	*sure=*
242	N:	*=then we took me and introduced me to her (and straight away)*
		the next day
243		*I started working (.) with her (.)the woman herself as I was*
244		*recommended b:y my friend .hh that she knew my friend*
245		*(2.3) she offered me (.) another job on week*
246		*ends I said yes I do them (.)then I practically*
247		*worked during the week (in the early hours of the morning)(.)and*
		Saturdays and Sundays
248		*I worked (1.2) and then from there I started to sort myself out*

TRANSLATION OF EXAMPLE 5. LILIANA – POST-2000 ARRIVAL [INTERVIEW 39]

80	L:	*Yes of course (.) I arrive in 40' more or less*
81	S:	*()*
82	L:	*Rest assured that I arrive and do it*
83	R:	*Is everything ok,*
84	L:	*Yes (.) I'm sorry but I'm going to have*
85		*to leave (.) it was my supervisor just*
86		*there's a thing at work and I have to lend a her a hand*
87	R:	*You work on Sundays,*
88	L:	*Normally no(.)but it appears that one of the cleaners is absent*
89	R:	*Aha*
90	L:	*The supervisor has helped me a lot*

TRANSLATION OF EXAMPLE 6. JULIO – POST-2000 ARRIVAL [INTERVIEW 40]

32 R: *How's your job,*
33 J: *Well good (.) my supervisor is a good person and*
34   *helps one out so when he asks me for something*
35   *I oblige*
36 R: *In what sense,*
37 J: *Well whatever he asks I do him a favour*
38 R: *What type of favours,*
39 J: *a cover because someone couldn't go to work at the last*
40   *minute (.) or: to clean something that a colleague*
41   *didn't do well to avoid complaints afterwards*
42 R: *Aha*
43 J: *And we:ll. In this way they bear you in mind*
44 R: *For what,*
45 J: *for other jobs and for the roster*

TRANSLATION OF EXAMPLE 7. ANA – 80S-ARRIVAL [INTERVIEW 33]

32 R: *Who do you recommend for jobs*
33 A: *Only people I know well*
34 R: *What is to know well,*
35 A: *Only people I trust*
36 R: *Trust,*
37 A: *for example relatives that you know work*
38   *well and will not do things badly <or those who*
39   *are not relatives but you know work well>*
40 R: *And how do you know they work well=*
41 A: *because I've seen them work (.) one's worked with*
42   *them or a person that you trust knows they are*
43   *good*
44 R: *What is to work well for you,*
45 A: *not to create problems(.) if they ask you to come up with stuff*
46   *saying oh no I only do (.) you have to work*
47   *conscientiously*

Appendix

TRANSLATION OF EXAMPLE 8. JOHAN – SECOND GENERATION [INTERVIEW 10]

22 R: *Would you recommend someone for a job*
23 J: *I'd have to have a very close relationship o:r (h)*
24   *know the person having seen how the person works*
25   *many times to see what the person (h) is like but the rest*
26   *no. HH no I wouldn't stick my neck out for them*
27   *as we say (.) one may end up looking bad*

TRANSLATION OF EXAMPLE 9. CATALINA 90S MIGRANT [INTERVIEW 13]

45 R: *Have you recommended anyone for a job,*
46 C: *Uff lots of times*
47 R: *For example,*
48   *Friends of friends, people I worked with*
49   *before but you have to be careful because they can*
50 C: *make you look bad*
51 R: *In what sense*
52 C: *Because they don't do their job well and then they make you*
53   *look bad in front of people.*
54 R: *Explain that a little to me*
55 C: *So you can no longer recommend anyone (.) they lose*
56   *trust in you*

TRANSLATION OF EXAMPLE 10. DARIO – 90S MIGRANT [INTERVIEW 15]		

268   R: *Aha very well .HH and: I know that you now have a business*
269   *Norma told me .HH*
270   D: *.hh yes now yes (now) I have my own:: (h) ()*
271   R: *You have your ow(n) comp[an-]*
272   D: *[com]pany*
273   R: *Your own company well done. HH and who helped you*
274   *to set up the company?*
275   D: *Hh M::(h) let's see::(h) u::(h) wit-u(h) this(h)*
276   *this(h) let's see () and I () they saw me*
277   *work I don't know::(h) and the way in which the people*
278   *I help find work works*
279   R: *Yes .HH*
280   D: *And::h) hh everything that came to me (.) came from nowhere*
281   *that is::(h) it was:(h) .HH (.) working well*
282   *speaking to the very people with the English themselves*
283   R: *Yes=*
284   D: *=u::(h) that created trust (h)*
285   R: *Mj(h)*
286   D: *that (came through) hh in the confidence*
287   *that .HH they gained (they saw-) that they gained in me*
288   R: *Mj(h)*
289   D: *And they opened that door and said (.) they told me*
290   *.HH why don't you work for us? (.)*
291   *directly . HH and that's (wh-) I opened the*
292   *Company*
293   R: *M:(h)=*
294   D: *=so things started to happ- I never (hh) u::(h)*
295   *(opened) (). .HH never: (h)knocked on doors (.)*
296   *each person called me(h) (.) ea- u:(h) small companies*
297   *started to () in that moment () (these gateways)*
298   *to offices*
299   R: *Aha*

TRANSLATION OF EXAMPLE 11. SUSANA – POST-2000 MIGRANT [INTERVIEW 1]

65	R:	*And in your experience how is work found*
66		*in London,*
67	S:	*U:(h) I think that um (.) everyone comes*
68		*with the same mentality (.) everyone has*
69		*different personal situations so for*
70		*example some people (0.4) that have*
71		*economic help for example from Colombia it's much*
72		*easier ()(.) the others from word of mouth*
74	R:	*=aha=*
75	S:	*=(I think) that they fall in love (with their work)*
76		*because) Colombians are very good*
78		*Working is a problem () in like organisations (.) .HH*
79		*that or you start clea:ning you start waitressing and you have*
80		*to pay () and you have to work*
81		*and-and- you cannot leave that job because and-and-that's it*
82		*you stay there it's very difficult to get out from there*
83		*(IT IS)(0.1). hh so I realised that*
84	R:	*°Yes°*
85	S:	*But we already (know) the environment (.) and::(h)*
86		*could help people as () although ()*
87		*it is: (.) the visa (.) and the work permit*
88	R:	*And how do they find work*
89	S:	*°from word of mouth°*

TRANSLATION OF EXAMPLE 12. SUSANA – POST-2000 MIGRANT [INTERVIEW 1]

CONTINUED

90 S: *In Colombia I mean (only like if you're my)*
91 *friend are you going to find work (0.1)HH but here:(h)*
92 *I recommend my friends () (I recommend them as*
93 *someone I kno<u>w</u>(.) but the process i:s entirely*
94 *their decision and: I've recommended some people> ()*
95 *who work and others that don't)<=*
96 R: *=and why do you think that happens*
97 S: *.HH I think that people are more-more (.)regular in*
98 *these type of things (and processes and people*
99 *sense it.)(.) I think that the English() that*
100 *I'm your friend doesn't mean that I work w<u>ell</u>(.)()*
101 *I like you but=*
102 R: *=and between Colombians?*
103 S: *() (.) because it's different if you go for a*
104 *a::a: cleaning job for example (.) you don't*
105 *need any kind of reference (.) .hh unless*
106 *They kn<u>ow</u> you (.)that they ask you if you know how to*
107 *clean? I didn't know but said I did because*
108 *you can mop a floor or clean a bathroom(.).hh*
109 *okey I know her u:(h)mh she is trustworthy (so that)*
110 *you can hire her () so it's: (.) it depends where*
111 *you are*

	TRANSLATION OF EXAMPLE 13. SUSANA CONTINUED [INTERVIEW 1]	
181	S:	*And what exactly is your project about*
182	R:	*It's for a book on relationships among*
183		*Latin Americans in London*
184	S:	*What?*
185	R:	*Specifically I'm interested in the topic of*
186		*palanca*
187	S:	*The palanca*(h)° (.) HHEHHEHHEHH
188	R:	*Yes.*
190	S:	*First (.) maybe you arrive to some*
191		*place and: (.) because you're Colombian*
192		*a Colombian hires someone who is Colombian*
193	R:	*A Colombian hires a Colombian=*
194	S:	*=I'd say so*
195	R:	*And why do you think this is the case*
196	S:	*(I think that it's because he knows (its people) ()*
197		*the learning processes of people they know how*
198		*how they work .HH and I think it's very difficult*
199		*for some people : (.) the interrelationship*
200		*With other cultures?*
201	R:	Mj(h)
202	S:	*So dealing with a (Pole) is different dealing*
203		*with a Spaniard is different*
204		*everyone has different learning processes*
205		*and working processes .HH and sometimes people*
206		*() the same (h). HH but in any case it depends*
207		*on your circle and your market*

TRANSLATION OF EXAMPLE 14. SUSANA CONTINUED [INTERVIEW 1]

208	R:	*Do you think palanca works here*
209	S:	*I think that recommendations work(h)*
210		*but: (H) (0.1) in these jobs (0.2)how can I say it*
211		*I (.) have(h) tried to help a lot of people a lot*
212		*of people (I have had to) () other () they tell*
213		*me that they appreciate me a lot °()it doesn't work*
214		*and () it works°(0.1) and it's fine and I accept it and*
215		*I really respect procedures and prefer it like this*
216		*so that (h) (0.4)I bring her you get to know her ()*
217		*but it's your decision if you hire her () hhhh=*
218	R:	*=right*
219	S:	*it's your head (hh) hhehh*
220		*=yes because well (you think that) and:(h)(.) there is*
221		*A risk there and it's (.)that you lose your capacity*
222		*to recommend another person*

TRANSLATION OF EXAMPLE 15. JUAN CARLOS – LATE-80S ARRIVAL [INTERVIEW 13]

88	R:	*do you hire people to work here?=*
89	C:	*=(sometimes)=*
90	R:	*=recommendees=*
91	C:	*=°(most of the time)°=*
92	R:	*=and what kind of people?=*
93	C:	*=Latinos*
94	R:	*Why Latinos?*
95	C:	*Because it's a Latin place*
96	R:	*Any preference?*
97	C:	*Colombians ()(.) Colom-=*
98	R:	*= and why Colombians?*
99	C:	*I know them (.)I relate well with them and they are*
100		*dynamic do you understand me? And they come*
101		*recommended*

References

Agha, A. (2007). *Language and Social Relations*. Cambridge: Cambridge University Press.

Ames, R. T. (2021). *Human Becomings: Theorizing Persons for Confucian Role Ethics*. New York: SUNY Press.

Anthias, F. (2007). Ethnic Ties: Social Capital and the Question of Mobilisability. *The Sociological Review*, 55(4), 788–805.

APPG. (2017). All-Party Parliamentary Group 2017. *Interim Report into Integration of Immigrants*. www.socialintegrationappg.org.uk.

Appadurai, A. (1996). *Modernity at Large: Cultural Dimensions of Globalization*. Minneapolis and London: University of Minnesota Press.

Archer, L., & Fitch, K. L. (1994). Communication in Latin American Multinational Organizations. In R. L. Wiseman and R. Shurer, eds., *Communicating in Multinational Organizations*. Thousand Oaks, CA: Sage, pp. 75–93.

Arundale, R. B. (2020). *Communicating & Relating*. New York: Oxford University Press.

Atkinson, R. (1998). *The Life Story Interview*. London: Sage.

Austin, J. L. (1961). *How to Do Things with Words*. Oxford: Oxford University Press.

Alexander, C. (2017). Beyond the 'The "Diaspora" Diaspora': A Response to Rogers Brubaker. *Ethnic and Racial Studies*, 40(9), 1544–1555.

Bakhtin, M. (1981). *The Dialogic Imagination: Four Essays*. Translated by M. Holquist. Austin, TX: University of Texas Press.

Bakewell, O., de Haas, H., & Kubal, A. (2012). Migration Systems, Pioneer Migrants, and the Role of Agency. *Journal of Critical Realism*, 11, 413–437.

Baum, T. (2015). Human Resources in Tourism: Still Waiting for Change? A 2015 reprise. *Tourism Management*, 50, 204–212. https://doi.org/10.1016/j.tourman.2015.02.001

Bendor, J., & Mookherjee, D. (1990). Norms, Third-Party Sanctions, and Cooperation. *Journal of Law, Economics, & Organization*, 6(1), 33–63.

Bendor, J., & Swistak, P. (2001). The Evolution of Norms. *The American Journal of Sociology*, 106(6), 1493–1545.

Berg, B. L. (2007). *Qualitative Research Methods for the Social Sciences*. Boston: Pearson Education.

Berg, M. L. (2019). Super-diversity, Austerity, and the Production of Precarity: Latin Americans in London. *Critical Social Policy*, 39(2), 184–204.

Blommaert, J., & Backus A. (2013). Superdiverse Repertoires and the Individual. In I. Saint-Georges, & J. J. Weber, eds., *Multilingualism and Multimodality: The Future of Education Research*. Rotterdam: Sense Publishers, pp. 11–32.

Bourdieu, P. (1986). The Forms of Capital. In J. Richardson, ed., *Handbook for Theory and Research for the Sociology of Education*. Westport, CT: Greenwood, pp. 241–258.

Bourdieu, P. (2007). *Sketch for a Self-Analysis*. Cambridge, MA: Polity.

Bourdieu, P., & Wacquant, L. (1992). *An Invitation to Reflexive Sociology*. Chicago: The University of Chicago Press.

Bousfield, D. (2008). *Impoliteness in Interaction*. Amsterdam: John Benjamins.

Boyd, M. (1989). Family and Personal Networks in International Migration: Recent Developments and New Agendas. *International Migration Review*, 23, 638–670.

Braun, V., & Clarke, V. (2006). Using Thematic Analysis in Psychology. *Qualitative Research in Psychology*, 3,77–101.

Briggs, C. (1986). *Learning How to Ask A Sociolinguistic Appraisal of the Role of the Interview in Social Science Research*. Cambridge: Cambridge University Press.

Brown, P., & Levinson, S. (1987). *Politeness: Some Universals in Language Use*. Cambridge: Cambridge University Press.

Brubaker, R. (2005). The 'Diaspora' Diaspora. *Journal of Ethnic and Racial Studies*, 28, 1–19.

Butler, J. (2012). Precarious Life, Vulnerability, and the Ethics of Cohabitation. *The Journal of Speculative Philosophy*, 26, 134–151.

Casey, L. (2016). *The Casey Review: A Review into Opportunity and Integration (London)*. www.gov.uk/government/uploads/system/uploads/attachment_data/file/575973/The_Casey_Review_Report.pdf (last accessed February 2017)

Castles, S., & Davidson, A. (2020). *Citizenship and Migration: Globalization and the Politics of Belonging*. New York: Routledge.

Chamberlayne, P., Rustin, M., & Wengraf, T. eds., (2002). *Biography and Social Exclusion in Europe: Experiences and Life Journeys*. Bristol: The Policy Press.

CLAUK. (2021). Voicing the Collective Interests of the Latin American Community in the UK. www.clauk.org.uk/.

Coleman, J. (1988). Social Capital in the Creation of Human Capital. *American Journal of Sociology*, 94, S95–S120.

Coleman, J. (1990). *Foundations of Social Theory*. Harvard: Harvard University Press.

Culpeper, J. (2011). *Impoliteness: Using Language to Cause Offence*. Cambridge: Cambridge University Press.

Culpeper, J. (2021). Sociopragmatics: Roots and Definition. In M. Haugh, D. Kádár and M. Terkourafi, eds., *The Cambridge Handbook of Sociopragmatics*. Cambridge: Cambridge University Press, pp. 15–29.

Culpeper, J., & Kytö, M. (2000). Data in Historical Pragmatics: Spoken Interaction (Re)cast as Writing. *Journal of Historical Pragmatics*, 1(2), 175–199.

Culpeper, J., & Haugh, M. (2021). The Metalinguistics of Offence in (British) English: A Corpus-Based Metapragmatic Approach. *Journal of Language Aggression and Conflict*, 9(2), 185–214.

Culpeper, J., & Tantucci, V. (2021). The Principle of (Im)politeness Reciprocity. *Journal of Pragmatics*, 175, 146–164.

Dana, L. P. (2007). *Handbook of Research on Ethnic Minority Entrepreneurship: A Co-evolutionary + View on Resource Management*. Cheltenham: Edward Elgar.

De Fina, A., & Perrino, S. (2011). Introduction: Interviews vs. 'Natural' Contexts: A False Dilemma. *Language in Society*, 40, 1–11.

de Haas, H., Castles, S., & Miller, M. J. (2020). *The Age of Migration*, 6th ed. London: Red Globe Press.

Drew, P. (2003). Precision and Exaggeration in Interaction. *American Sociological Review*, 68(6), 917–938.

Dwyer, P., & Brown, D. (2008). Accommodating 'Others'?: Housing Dispersed, Forced Migrants in the UK. *Journal of Social Welfare & Family Law*, 30(3), 203–218.

Dynel, M., & Poppi, F. (2019). Risum Teneatis, Amici?: The Socio-pragmatics of RoastMe Humour. *Journal of Pragmatics*, 139, 1–21.

Faraday, A., & Plummer, K. (1979). Doing Life Histories. *Sociological Review*, 27 (4), 773–798.

Fielding, N. (1981). *The National Front*. London: Routledge.

Fitch, K. (1998). Text and Context: A Problematic Distinction for Ethnographers. *Research on Language and Social Interaction*, 31, 91–107.

Fitzgerald, R., & Housley, W., eds., (2015). *Advances in Membership Categorization Analysis*. London: Sage.

Fox, J. E., & Jones, D. (2013). Migration, Everyday Life and the Ethnicity Bias. *Ethnicities*, 13, 385–400.

Garcés-Conejos Blitvich, P. (2022). Moral Emotions, Good Moral Panics, Social Regulation, and Online Public Shaming. *Language & Communication*, 84, 61–75.

García, C. (2016). De-Westernizing Public Relations: A Comparative Analysis of Culture and Economics Structure in China and Mexico. *Asian Pacific Relations Journal*, 17(2), 9–27.

García, O. (2009). *Bilingual Education in the 21st Century: A Global Perspective.* Oxford: Blackwell.

García, O., & Li, W. (2014). *Translanguaging: Language, Bilingualism, and Education.* London: Palgrave Macmillan.

Giddens, A. (1990). *The Consequences of Modernity.* Stanford: Stanford University Press.

Goebel, Z. (2015). Establishing Believability in Interviews. *Tilburg Papers in Culture Studies*, 140.

Goffman, E. (1967). *Interaction Ritual: Essays on Face-to-Face Behaviour.* New York: Doubleday.

Goldstein, T. (1997). *Two Languages at Work: Bilingual Life on the Production Floor.* New York: Mouton de Gruyter.

Granovetter, M. (1995). *Getting a Job. A Study of Contacts and Careers.* Chicago: University of Chicago Press.

Greenbank, E., & Marra, M. (2020). Addressing Societal Discourses: Negotiating an Employable Identity as a Former Refugee. *Language and Intercultural Communication*, 20(2), 110–124.

Grice, H. P. (1975). *Logic and Conversation.* In P. Cole, & J. L. Morgan. (Eds.), *Syntax and Semantics*, Vol. 3, Speech Acts (pp. 41–58). New York: Academic Press.

Guarnizo, L., & Portés, A. (1991). Tropical Capitalists: U.S.-Bound Immigration and Small Enterprise Development in the Dominican Republic. In S. Díaz-Briquets, & S. Weintraub, eds., *Migration, Remittances, and Small Business Development, Mexico and Caribbean Basin Countries.* Boulder: Westview Press, pp. 101–131.

Gumperz, J. (1972/1986). Introduction. In J. Gumperz, & D. Hymes, eds., *Directions in Sociolinguistics: The Ethnography of Communication.* London: Blackwell, pp. 1–25.

Gumperz, J. (1982). *Discourse Strategies.* Cambridge: Cambridge University Press.

Hall, S. (1990). Cultural Identity and Diaspora. In J. Rutherford, ed., *Identity: Community, Culture, Difference.* London: Lawrence and Wishart, pp. 222–237.

Haugh, M. (2022). (Online) Public Denunciation, Everyday Incivilities and Offence. *Language & Communication*, 84, 44–59.

Haugh, M., Kádár, D., & Terkourafi M., eds., (2021). *The Cambridge Handbook of Sociopragmatics.* Cambridge: Cambridge University Press.

Holmes, J., & Marra, M. (2017). You're a Proper Tradesman Mate: Identity Struggles and Workplace Transitions in New Zealand. In D. van de Mieroop, & S. Schnurr, eds., *Identity Struggles: Evidence from Workplaces Around the World.* Amsterdam: John Benjamins, pp. 127–146.

Horgan, M. (2021). Sacred Civility? An Alternative Conceptual Architecture Informed by Cultural Sociology. *Journal of Politeness Research*, 17(1), 9–34.

Huschke, S. (2014). Fragile Fabric: Illegality Knowledge, Social Capital and Health-Seeking of Undocumented Latin American Migrants in Berlin. *Journal of Ethnic and Migration Studies*, 40(12), 2010–2029.

Hyland, K. (2017). Metadiscourse: What Is It and Where Is It Going? *Journal of Pragmatics*, 113, 16–29.

International Labour Organization (ILO). (2010). *International Labour Migration: A Rights-Based Approach*. Geneva: International labour office. www.ilo.org/wcmsp5/groups/public/–dgreports/–dcomm/documents/publication/wcms_125362.pdf.

International Organization for Migration (IOM). (2010). *International Dialogue on Migration Intersessional Workshop on Migration and Transnationalism: Opportunities and Challenges*, 9–10 March. www.iom.int/sites/default/files/jahia/webdav/shared/shared/mainsite/microsites/IDM/workshops/migration_and_transnationalism_030910/background_paper_en.pdf.

International Organization for Migration (IOM). (2021). *Toolkit for Integrating Migration into Employment*. Brussels: IOM. https://eea.iom.int/sites/g/files/tmzbdl666/files/mmicd/employment_toolkit.pdf.

Jones, R. (2020). The Rise of the Pragmatic Web: Implications for Rethinking Meaning and Interaction. In C. Tagg, & M. Evans, eds., *Historicising the Digital: English Language Practices in New and Old Media*. Berlin: de Gruyter Mouton, pp. 17–37. https://doi.org/10.1515/9783110670837-003.

Jucker, A., & Taavitsainen, I., eds., (2010). *Historical Pragmatics*. Berlin/New York: De Gruyter Mouton.

Kádár, D., & Márquez Reiter, R. (2015). (Im)politeness and (Im)morality: Insights from Intervention. *Journal of Politeness Research: Language, Behavior, Culture*, 11(2), 239–260.

Kirilova, M., & Angouri, J. (2017). Communication Practices and Policies in Workplace Mobility. In S. Canagarajah, ed., *The Routledge Handbook of Migration and Language*. London: Routledge, pp. 540–557.

Laidlaw, J. (2010). Agency and Responsibility: Perhaps You Can Have Too Much of a Good Thing. In M. Lambek, ed., *Ordinary Ethics: Anthropology, Language, and Action*. New York: Fordham University Press, pp. 143–164.

Lambek, M. (2015). Living as if It Mattered. In M. Lambek, V. Das, D. Fassin, & W. Keane, eds., *Four Lectures on Ethics: Anthropological Perspectives*. Chicago: HAU Books, The University of Chicago Press, pp. 5–52.

Lave, J., & Wenger, E. (1991). *Situated Learning: Legitimate Peripheral Participation.* Cambridge: Cambridge University Press.

Ledeneva, A. (2008). Blat and Guanxi: Informal Practices in Russia and China. *Comparative Studies in Society and History,* 50(1), 118–144.

Levinson, S. (1983). *Pragmatics.* Cambridge: Cambridge University Press.

Lincoln, Y. S., & Guba, E. G. (1985). *Naturalistic Inquiry.* Newbury Park, CA: Sage.

Lindsley, S. L., & Braithwaite, C. A. (2006). 'You Should Wear a Mask': Facework Norms in Cultural and Intercultural Conflict in Maquiladoras. *International Journal of Intercultural Relations,* 20(2), 199–225.

Lomnitz, L. A. (1971). Reciprocity of Favors in the Urban Middle Class of Chile. *Studies in Economic Anthropology,* AS7, 93–106.

Lomnitz, L. A. (1977). *Networks and Marginality: Life in a Mexican Shantytown.* New York: Academic Press.

Locher, M. A., & Graham, S. L. (2010). Introduction to Interpersonal Pragmatics. In M. A. Locher, & S. L. Graham, eds., *Interpersonal Pragmatics.* Berlin: Mouton, pp. 1–13.

Locher, M. A., & Watts, R. J. (2008). Relational Work and Impoliteness: Negotiating Norms of Linguistic Behaviour. *Language Power and Social Process,* 21, 77–99.

Lorenzo-Dus, N., Garcés-Conejos Blitvich, P., & Bou-Franch, P. (2011). On-line Polylogues and Impoliteness: The Case of Postings Sent in Response to the Obama Reggaeton YouTube Video. *Journal of Pragmatics,* 43, 2578–2593.

Márquez Reiter, R. (2018). Interviews as Sites of Ideological Work. *Spanish in Context,* 15, 54–76.

Márquez Reiter, R. (2021). How Can Ethnography Contribute to Understanding (Im)politeness? *Journal of Politeness Research,* 17(1), 35–59.

Márquez Reiter, R. (2022). Translocalisation of Values, Relationality and Offence. *Language & Communication,* 84, 20–32.

Márquez Reiter, R. (2023). Mobility and Stasis: Migrant Portraits from a Madrid Market. In R. Márquez Reiter and A. Patiño-Santos, eds., *Language Practices and Processes among Latin Americans in Europe.* London: Routledge, 25–49.

Márquez Reiter, R., & Kádár, D. (2022). Sociality and Moral Conflicts: Migrant Stories of Relational Vulnerability. *Pragmatics and Society,* 13(1), 1–21.

Márquez Reiter, R., & Martín Rojo, L. (2015). The Dynamics of (Im)Mobility. (In)Transient Capitals and Linguistic Ideologies among Latin American Migrants in London and Madrid. In R. Márquez Reiter, & L. Martín Rojo, eds., *A Sociolinguistics of Diaspora: Latino Practices, Identities and Ideologies.* New York: Routledge, pp. 83–101.

Márquez Reiter, R., & Patiño-Santos, A. (2017). The Discursive Construction of Moral Agents among Successful Economic Migrants in Elephant & Castle, London. *Tilburg Papers in Culture Studies*, Paper 194.

Márquez Reiter, R., & Patiño-Santos, A. (2021). The Politics of Conviviality: On the Ground Experiences from Spanish-Speaking Latin Americans in Elephant & Castle, London. *Journal of Sociolinguistics*, 25(5), 662–681.

Márquez Reiter, R., & Paz, A. (2013). Curated Presidential Conversation. *Society for Linguistic Anthropology*, 112th AAA Annual Meeting, Chicago IL, 20–24 November.

Massey, D. S., Arango, J., Hugo, G. et al. (1993). Theories of International Migration: A Review and Appraisal. *Population and Development Review*, 19(3), 431–466.

Massey, D. S., Arango, J., Hugo, G. et al. (1998). *Worlds in Motion: Understanding International Migration at the End of the Millennium*. Oxford: Clarendon Press.

Maton, K. (2003). Pierre Bourdieu and Epistemic Conditions of Social Scientific Knowledge. *Space & Culture*, 6(1), 52–65.

McIlwaine, C., & Bunge, D. (2016). *Towards Visibility: The Latin American Community in London*. London: Trust for London.

McIlwaine, C., & Bunge, D. (2019). Onward Precarity, Mobility, and Migration Among Latin Americans in London. *Antipode*, 51(2), 601–619.

McIlwaine, C., Cock, J. C., & Linneker, B. (2011). *No Longer Invisible*. London: Queen Mary University.

Mills, S. (2017). *English Politeness and Class*. Cambridge: Cambridge University Press.

Molm, L. (2003). Theoretical Comparisons of Forms of Exchange. *Sociological Theory*, 21,1–17.

Mouw, T. (2003). Social Capital and Finding a Job: Do Contacts Matter? *American Sociological Review*, 68, 868–898.

Nitsch, M., & Diebel, F. (2007). Guanxi Economics: Confucius Meets Lenin, Keynes, and Schum- peter in Contemporary China. *Revista de Administração Pública*, 41(5), 959–992.

Office for National Statistics. (2011). *Language in England and Wales*. www.ons.gov.uk/peoplepopulationandcommunity/culturalidentity/language/articles/languageinenglandandwales/2013-03-04.

O'Reilly, K. (2009). *Sampling: Key Concepts in Ethnography*. London: Sage.

O'Rourke, J., & Tuleja, E. (2009). *Intercultural Communication for Business: Managerial Communication Series*. Ohio, USA: South-Western Cengage Learning.

Ordoñez Bustamante, D., & Sousa de Barbieri, L. (2003). *El Capital Ausente.* Lima, Perú: Tetis, Graf.

Ortner, S. B. (2016). Dark Anthropology and Its Others: Theory Since the Eighties. *HAU: Journal of Ethnographic Theory,* 6(1), 47–73.

Paulus, T. M., & Wise, A. F. (2019). *Looking for Insight, Transformation, and Learning in Online Talk.* New York: Routledge.

Patiño-Santos, A., & Márquez Reiter, R. (2019). Banal Interculturalism: Latin Americans in Elephant & Castle. *Language and Intercultural Communication,* 19, 227–241.

Portes, A. (1998). Social Capital: Its Origins and Applications in Modern Sociology. *Annual Review of Sociology,* 24, 1–24.

Putnam, R. D. (1995). Bowling Alone: America's Declining Social Capital. *Journal of Democracy,* 6(1), 65–78.

Roberts, B. (2014). Biographical Research: Past, Present, Future. In M. O'Neill, B. Roberts, & A. Sparkes, eds., Advances in Biographical Methods. London: Routledge, pp. 31–49.

Roth, W. D. (2016). The Multiple Dimensions of Race. *Ethnic and Racial Studies,* 39(8), 1310–1338.

Senft, G. (2014). *Understanding Pragmatics.* Routledge: London.

Sheller, M., & Urry, J., eds., (2004). *Tourism Mobilities: Places to Play, Places in Play.* London: Routledge.

Sheller, M., & Urry, J. (2006). The New Mobilities Paradigm. *Environment and Planning A: Economy and Space,* 38, 207–226.

Silverstein, M. (2003). Indexical Order and the Dialectics of Sociolinguistic Life. *Language & Communication,* 23(3–4), 193–229.

Spradley, J. (1980). *Participant Observation.* New York: Holt, Rinehart and Winston.

Starr, P. M. (2003). Making Public Relations Personal: An Exploratory Study of the Implications of Palanca and Guanxi on International Public Relations (Thesis). Stockton, CA: University of the Pacific, Department of Communication.

Stepputat, F., & Nyberg Sørensen, N. (2014). Sociology and Forced Migration. In E. Fiddian-Qasmiyeh, G. Loescher, K. Long, & N. Sigona, eds., *The Oxford Handbook of Refugees and Forced Migration Studies.* Oxford Handbooks Online https://doi.10.1093/oxfordhb/9780199652433.013.0036.

Sumption, M., & Walsh, W. (2022). *EU Migration to and from the UK.* Migration Observatory Briefing, COMPAS, University of Oxford, February 2022.

Thomas, J. (1983). Cross-Cultural Pragmatic Failure. *Applied Linguistics,* 4(2), 91–112.

Thompson, S., Fox, B., & Couper-Khulen, E. (2015). *Grammar in Everyday Talk: Building Responsive Actions*. Cambridge: Cambridge University Press.

Urciuoli, B. (2016). The Compromised Pragmatics of Diversity. *Language & Communication*, 15, 30–39.

Verschueren, J. (2008). Intercultural Communication and the Challenges of Migration. *Language and Intercultural Communication*, 8, 21–35.

Verschueren, J. (2021). Reflexivity and Meta-awareness. In M. Haugh, D. Kádár, & M. Terkourafi, eds., *The Cambridge Handbook of Sociopragmatics*. Cambridge: Cambridge University Press, pp. 117–139.

Vertovec, S. (2007). Super-diversity and Its Implications. *Ethnic and Racial Studies*, 30(6), 1024–1054.

Vigouroux, C. (2013). Informal Economy and Language Practice in the Context of Migrations. In A. Duchêne, M. Melissa, & C. Roberts eds., *Language, Migration and Social Inequalities: A Critical Sociolinguistic Perspective on Institutions and Work*. Bristol: Multilingual Matter, pp. 296–328.

Vivanco, L. (2018). *A Dictionary of Cultural Anthropology*. Oxford: Oxford University Press.

Vollmer, B. (2011). *Irregular Migration in the UK: Definitions, Pathways, Scale*. Migration Observatory Briefing, COMPAS, University of Oxford, July 2011.

Vološinov, V. (1929/1973). *Marxism and the Philosophy of Language*. Translated by Ladislav Matejka & Irwin R. Titunik, Cambridge, MA: Harvard University Press.

Wacquant, L. J. D. (1989). For a Socio-analysis of Intellectuals: On Homo Academicus. *Berkeley Journal of Sociology*, 34, 1–29.

Wessendorf, S. (2017). Being New and Unconnected: Pioneer Migrants in London. *MMG Working Paper* 17-01. Göttingen: Max Planck Institute for the Study of Religious and Ethnic Diversity.

White, A., & Ryan, L. (2008). Polish 'Temporary' Migration: The Formation and Significance of Social Networks. *Europe-Asia Studies*, 60, 1467–1502.

Wills, J., Datta, K., Evans, Y. et al. (2010). *Global Cities at Work: New Migrant Divisions of Labour*. London: Pluto Press.

Wortham, S., Mortimer, K., Lee, K., Allard, E., & While, K. D. (2011). Interviews as Interactional Data. *Language in Society*, 40, 39–50.

Yuval-Davis, N. (2013). A Situated Intersectional Everyday Approach to the Study of Bordering. Working Paper No. 2. *Euroborderscapes*. European Commission.

Zalpa, G., Tapia Tovar, E., & Reyes Martínez, J. (2014). 'El que a buen árbol se arrima . . . ' intercambio de favores y corrupción. *Cultura y representaciones sociales*. 9(17), 149–176.

Cambridge Elements ≡

Pragmatics

Jonathan Culpeper
Lancaster University, UK

Jonathan Culpeper is Professor of English Language and Linguistics in the Department of Linguistics and English Language at Lancaster University, UK. A former co-editor-in-chief of the *Journal of Pragmatics* (2009–2014), with research spanning multiple areas within pragmatics, his major publications include *Impoliteness: Using Language to Cause Offence* (2011, CUP) and *Pragmatics and the English Language* (2014, Palgrave; with Michael Haugh).

Michael Haugh
University of Queensland, Australia

Michael Haugh is Professor of Linguistics and Applied Linguistics in the School of Languages and Cultures at the University of Queensland, Australia. A former co-editor-in-chief of the *Journal of Pragmatics* (2015–2020), with research spanning multiple areas within pragmatics, his major publications include *Understanding Politeness* (2013, CUP; with Dániel Kádár), *Pragmatics and the English Language* (2014, Palgrave; with Jonathan Culpeper), and *Im/politeness Implicatures* (2015, Mouton de Gruyter).

Advisory Board

About the Series

The Cambridge Elements in Pragmatics series showcases dynamic and high-quality original, concise and accessible scholarly works. Written for a broad pragmatics readership it encourages dialogue across different perspectives on language use. It is a forum for cutting-edge work in pragmatics: consolidating theory (especially through cross-fertilization), leading the development of new methods, and advancing innovative topics in pragmatics.

Cambridge Elements ☰

Pragmatics

Elements in the Series

Printed in the United States
by Baker & Taylor Publisher Services

Printed in the United States
by Baker & Taylor Publisher Services